The ENORMOU

Book of Talk For Writing Games For KS2

Introduction

The Enormous Book of Talk for Writing Games for KS2 is a handbook for teachers (but can be used at home too), to improve children's writing skills through engaging them with speaking and drama activities. Retelling stories, drawing on a bank of known tales and creating new stories orally acts as a powerful influence on children's writing. Too often, they are rushed into writing a story before having tools in their kit to do so. Once children are confident in speaking creatively, their writing flows more easily. Games in this book will help achieve this ease and develop their imaginations.

How to Use this Book

- Some games are harder than others, but you will know which will best suit your class. Even if the children find a game difficult at first, persevere, especially if they are not used to drama or speaking aloud.
- Some of the games give you an opportunity to use subjects or stories you have been learning in class, within the game itself.
- Feel free to add to this repertoire of tried and tested games with your own ideas that you come up with along the way.

The book is split into six units, detailed below. We have suggested equipment that you will need, the skills the game develops and how to vary and advance the game. We have used simple fairy tales as examples in some games as these are familiar reference points. However, these games can be adapted and related to the story that you are working on in class. It is also worth considering which games are needed to help the children deepen their understanding of a story or develop their own versions. What does the story demand – and what do the children need?

1. Warm-up Games

These games are perfect for starting a session. They are there to loosen the imagination, eradicate any sense of anxiety that might hinder creative thought and to involve everyone, grabbing attention. They encourage the children to be confident when contributing their ideas, speaking and creating aloud.

2. Imitation Games

Imitation is the first stage of 'talk for writing'. It is when a child becomes very familiar with a story, so that they are able to retell it 'word-for-word' or in their own words. They then have a story pattern in their head that they know really well, which can be used as a springboard to innovation and invention. In a wider sense, imitation concerns getting to know the plot, themes and characters of a story really well, so games in this section will focus on enhancing those aspects too. Imitation builds a child's imaginative world, provides them with banks of vocabulary, sentence and text patterns. It is like creating a living library in a child's mind. The games also focus on helping children to deepen their understanding of the story.

3. Innovation Games

Innovation is the second stage of 'talk for writing'. It is when children create their own version of a well-known story. This is rather like a 'story bridge' that helps children move towards inventing by themselves. The games provide simple ways to innovate through to more complex approaches. Innovation is about manipulating a story you already know.

4. Invention Games

Invention is the third stage of 'talk for writing'. This is the ability to create something new, drawing on the children's inner world of stories, their own lives, their reading and their ability to manipulate stories and create something for themselves. It is a form of intensive play where we dig deep and find our own characters and tales.

5. Poetry Starters

There is a very brief section of suggested poetry 'starters'. With the children, invent other ideas that can be used in a similar way. They will encourage creative ideas and help children to learn how to use words powerfully, as well as developing skill with alliteration and imagery.

6. Story Bank

The book ends with a bank of stories, which we have referred to in the book and on the audio CD. Accompanying the stories are some helpful teaching notes.

The Audio CD & Image CD

The audio CD was recorded in the winter at home. We played some of the games as well as reading a few stories. Check the teaching notes and then try using our recording as a way into a story and games with the children. In this book, wherever you see this symbol, it means the game is played on the CD.

There is also an image CD with a bank of images to use with some of the activities. You will need this whenever you see this symbol.

A Note about Teaching Drama

For some teachers, the idea of 'drama' fills them with unnecessary dread. Don't worry – we are not asking you to organise the nativity or class assembly, it is all much simpler than that!

Drama comes naturally to all humans. Every day, we engage with drama – we improvise our lives, making up what we're going to say and do, moment to moment. We use persuasive techniques to get what we want. We recount stories to friends over coffee. These are the roots of drama. At its simplest, drama is about pretending to be someone else and imagining new situations.

Of course, children are the most natural actors of all because drama is a form of play, and what children like to do best is play. I have an eight-year-old friend, Isabella. Despite being a sassy South London kid, she loves to appoint me 'Inspector' and, in role as 'Headmistress', show me around her Playmobil school, making the small figures come to life. Sometimes we record funny interviews on her Dad's iPhone and she pretends to be a famous Professor or author. Once she showed me all the different characters she could transform into with the scarf she was wearing ('an old crone, an American lady driving in an open top car...'). Playing like this is the start of drama and inventing your own stories and characters.

All children love to play games and create stories even if they do not read widely. I used to teach drama to a group of boys in North London who didn't read as much as Isabella. Nevertheless, every lesson they would beg to 'go on an adventure' and I would find myself being handed an imaginary rifle and cowboy hat, ready to take part in a great train robbery. Though I would have preferred less imaginary guns, it was thrilling to spend forty minutes interacting in this way. Drama is simply an extension of what children do quite naturally.

So, how to teach it? One trick is to try as much as possible not to appear as though you are teaching it! It's almost non-teaching, pretending it isn't a lesson, so the learning is natural. The more the children's self-consciousness is taken away, the better, as this can spoil the drama. For this to happen, you have to play the games with them, in role. If you strongly commit to what you're doing, suspend disbelief, then your class will commit. As teacher, you must be in role too, as characters, engaging with the games. By being in role, you can employ a teacher's subterfuge, manipulating the drama. Play some games every day, so it becomes a natural part of the children's routine. Some of them take less than five minutes. There is always room for one at the start of the day.

Plan a lesson that suits the children and story that you are studying. You know your class. Adapt the games in the book to suit their level and experience. Remember mistakes are alright, as you only learn and improve because of them. As you can hear on the CD, some of these games are hard for adults too! In the great dramatist Samuel Beckett's prose piece *Worstward Ho*, he states 'Ever failed. No matter. Try again. Fail again. Fail better.' It's useful to keep this in mind. Accept and consider all ideas offered by your pupils. Once you all know the games well, playing them will become easier and I expect your class will have 'favourite games' that they will want to play again and again!

Try to make the playing space as special as you can for the children. A story area, wearing a special story cloak, having a story chest with costumes and props, all help to encourage excitement around the games. If the game is quite a physical one, make sure that there is enough space to play and that the area is safe.

Drama is vital to encourage in schools. Research demonstrates that it improves creativity, confidence, communication and social development. It can be used across the curriculum, to liven up every lesson and to help children gain a different perspective on a subject, perhaps illuminating something they found difficult before. Do not leave it for 'the school play', or 'the class talk'. Use it where you can. Imagine how much fun a science lesson could be if a child, dressed in a lab coat and goggles, explains an experiment by pretending to be a professor interviewed for a television documentary.

I have played these games with children and professional actors – very enjoyably and successfully with both. I hope you and your class enjoy playing these games as much as I do!

Poppy

Track List

1. Hello
2. Introduction to Creative Word Games
3. Word List Race
4. The Synonym Race
5. The Wizard's Suitcase
6. I Must Have Been Dreaming, But...
7. Introduction to Imitation Games
8. Ping Pong Tales
9. I Can See...
10. Gossiping Over the Gate
11. Phone a Friend
12. Agony Aunt/Uncle
13. Introduction to Innovation Games
14. Yo-Yo Tales
15. Story Swapping
16. Embellish
17. Alteration
18. Changing the Genre
19. Viewpoint
20. Introduction to Invention Games
21. Pie and Poppy's Perhaps Game
22. Impossible Suggestions
23. Ping Pong Connectives
24. The Salty Umbrella
25. The Story Restaurant
26. Stanislavski's Questions
27. In a Dark, Dark House
28. Who Will Buy?
29. Introduction to Poetry Starters
30. Poetry Starters
31. Introduction to Stories
32. Jack and the Beanstalk
33. The Pied Piper of Hamelin
34. Too High – The Story of Icarus
35. Midas
36. Goodbye!

Image List

Animals
Bee on flower
Black cat
Butterfly
Cat lying down
Cat sleeping
Cat's face
Cats
Close-up of camels
Close-up of elephant
Close-up of turkey
Cow's face
Dog on boat
Donkey
Elephant
Exotic bird
Frog
Gecko
Giraffes
Goat
Herd of elephants
Horses in snow
Kangaroo
Kitten with bowl of milk
Ladybirds
Ostrich
Rhinos
Sheep with lambs
Sheep
Siamese cat
Sitting cats
Swans
Tortoises
Wolf footprint in snow

Characters
Baby
Boy in cave
Boy looking out of window
Boy on British beach
Children walking on spit
Diving robot
Eyes
Group of old men sitting on bench
Group of Thai people
Lone man looking out at water
Man above Grand Canyon
Man contemplating
Man on American street
Man with laden donkey
Men throwing bales
Mountaineer
Old lady on bench
Old lady

Saxophone player
Scarecrow
Street dancer
Woman on tropical beach
Young man

Events

Beach anglers
Birthday
Boy preparing to dive into sea
Concert
Crash
Dancers
Deep snow
Dumped sofa and car
Fireworks
Fishing on Nile
Flood
Flooded bridge
Halloween
Men chatting
Motorbike rally
Olympic stadium
On stage
People in river
Punch and Judy show
Shipwreck
Snowman with igloo
Steam train
Street scene
Tea time
Waiting for school
Walking home
Wedding 2
Wedding
Woman serving food

Objects

Autumnal leaves
Ball
Bicycle
Boat
Boats
Cameras
Car
Carpet
Chest
Chilli peppers
Clock
Compass
Crystal ball
Dandelion
Decorated pebble
Diamond
Dice and chess board
Door
Dragon statue

Dragon's head
Face carved from stone
Fish hanging on line
Flip-flops
Fossil
Glove
Hats
Holly leaves
Ice cream
Lantern
Lollipops
Mannequin
Mobile phones
Moon
Peppers
Pumpkin
Red shoe
Rusty car
Sailing ship
Scarecrow fox
Shooting star
Steam train
Strawberries
Teddy bear
Telephone box
Telephone
Tractor
Trunks
Typewriter
Vehicle art
Watch, keys and book
Window
Wrought iron gate

Settings

Agricultural landscape
Attic room
Autumn
Beach dwellings
Beach
Beech trees
Blackberry bush
Blue lagoon
Castle
Castle ruins
Cave dwellings
Caves
Close-up of poppy
Clouds
Dawn
Desert
Distant cottage and lane
Dockside with cranes
Fairground
Field of flowers
Figure in tunnel
Garden seen through arch
Glass-domed roof

Grandma's kitchen
Graveyard in snow
Haunted house
Hobbit hut 1
Hobbit hut 2
Illuminated night sky
Jungle
Lake at dusk
Lake with reeds
Lighthouse
Looking up at trees
Magical forest
Manhattan skyline by night
Misty hill scene
Misty hollow
Moss on mill stone
Mountain
Peeling walls and ceiling
Person on bridge
Pier
Playground 2
Playground
Poppies
Railway track
Rickety bridge over water
Rocky river
Ruin
Shack
Shoe house
Silhouette of tree
Snowy track
Street by night
Sunbeams through church window
Sunlit graveyard
Sunset over sea
Tower in snow
Toy shop
Train station
Trees in mist
Under the pier
Woodland walk
Workshop
Wreck

UNIT 1: WARM-UP GAMES

1. Word Racing – Back to Back Letter 📷

For the whole class organised into pairs or small groups.

Equipment:
- the image CD and an interactive whiteboard
- a whiteboard and a whiteboard pen for you
- paper and pencils or mini whiteboards and whiteboard pens for the children
- dictionaries for the children to share
- a timer (if desired)

Skills Developed:
- creating word chains with matching start and end letters
- generating words with a constraint

How to Play the Game

The idea is that a child starts with any word, e.g. *cattle* and then their partner or the next player in their group has to say a word that starts with the last letter, e.g. *endless*. You might like to model this first on the whiteboard before the children continue the game in their pairs or groups. Use an image from the image CD to trigger the first word. A string of words might go like this.

Example
Cattle
Endless
Sunny
Yes
Sand
Dolphin...

You can continue like this for as long as desired. If you would like to introduce a competitive element to the game, give each pair or team a set time limit to come up with as many words as possible following the above rules. They will need to write each word down so that they can be counted at the end of the game. The winning pair or team are the players with the most words at the end of the allotted time period.

Variation
- An alternative to this game is to come up with words that start and end with the same letters:

    - toasted/treated
    - pull/pail
    - sound/sad

2. Word List Race – On a Topic 💿 📷

For the whole class.

Equipment:
- the audio CD and a CD player
- a whiteboard and a whiteboard pen for you
- paper and pencils or mini whiteboards and whiteboard pens for the children
- a timer
- the image CD and an interactive whiteboard (for the Variation)

Skills Developed:
- generating ideas around a topic (word association)
- becoming used to speaking aloud and sharing ideas

How to Play the Game

Begin by listening to the game being played on the CD. In many ways, this game is fundamental to all writing. It is played as a race. Give the children one minute to write down as many words as possible that they can think of associated with a given topic. So if the topic is 'snow' a child might write: *cold, wet, white, bare, snowflake, sparkle, blank, frail, fragile, crisp, crunchy, frosty, shiver, quiver, drift, fall, moths, flutter, wings, camouflage, transform...*

At first the children might find it hard to think of words. This is probably because they are thinking cognitively – and actually, the secret is to visualise the topic, hold it in their minds and inspect it carefully from all angles, bringing all their senses, thoughts, memories and feelings to that topic. What does it look like, how does it move, how would it feel? But also how do they *feel* about it, what memories do they have associated with the word?

Some classes need to start by doing this as a whole class with you rapidly jotting down their ideas on the whiteboard. If you do this every day for several weeks, you will find that the children improve their ability to generate words and can then play the game as a race.

Once children have had lots of practice with this game with you writing down their words, they can start to make their own lists. You may find that sometimes words come singly, but at other times words come in pairs or phrases.

Example
Topic word: Bonfire

Flames flickering
Red
Scarlet
Night
Smoke
Wood crackles

Variations

- Play the game in pairs. Divide the class into pairs with each child in each pair taking turns to say or write the next word or phrase. The pair that manages to think of the most words associated with a topic wins.

- Develop the game so that you play it in a circle. Choose a topic (one to do with a story you are studying would be best). Sit the children in a circle. Go round the circle and one-by-one invite each child to add something to the list, thinking up as many things to do with the topic as possible. How many times can you get round the circle before you run out of ideas? So if your topic is 'fruits', children might come up with: *apples, mangoes, strawberries, gooseberries,* etc. Start with simple, general topics, then be more specific, e.g. *things I could use to escape from a dragon.* Add a competitive element to the game by timing how long it takes to complete the circle. Next time, can the class think of words quicker and complete the circle in a faster time?

- Try using an image from the CD and brainstorm words that describe the picture. These could be shared or contributed to a class list. Then use these to write a description.

3. Word Racing – No Association 📷

For the whole class.

Equipment:

- a whiteboard and a whiteboard pen for you (if you want to record the words)
- the image CD and an interactive whiteboard (for the Variation)

Skills Developed:

- generating ideas
- developing the imagination

How to Play the Game

This is a fun game once the children become skilled at 'word racing.' It is a simple warm-up activity that gets the class used to generating ideas and ignites their imaginations. Ask the children to sit in a circle, then go round the circle and say a word, or a phrase aloud. The only rule of the game is that the word must in no way relate to the previous word. Each player must choose a word that has nothing to do with the word chosen before it.

Example
Orange
Spiders
Bedroom
Thailand
Alex
Sunlight
Soap
Dove

A player can challenge another (by shouting *challenge!*) to suggest that there is an association between words. For instance, in the example above, a challenge might be raised that there is a brand of soap called 'Dove.'

Variations

- Play the game in a line with each child adding the next word. If children lack confidence, ask them to work in pairs and set one pair against another, each pair taking a turn to say the next word. It can help if the children make a list of random words before they play the game or use the images on the CD to help with this. Then they can choose words from their list to use in the game.

- Follow the instructions for the main game, but instead of random words, each child has to say a connective for a story (*so, and, because, then, next,* etc.) or think up openings to stories (*one day there lived a man; early one morning; once upon a time,* etc.).

- Try getting the children to play the game in pairs. One child comes up with a word and then the other has to think of an antonym (opposite) for that word. This child then suggests a new word and the other child must think of the opposite to this.

Example
Good/Evil
Mean/Kind
Hope/Despair
Lost/Found
Guilty/Innocent

4. The Synonym Race 💿
For the whole class organised into pairs.

Equipment:
- the audio CD and a CD player
- a thesaurus for you to prepare the game
- paper and pencils or mini whiteboards and whiteboard pens for the children
- a timer (if desired)
- materials to make synonym posters for display and for the children's own journals

Skills Developed:
- generating alternative words with the same meaning

How to Play the Game
Introduce the game by listening to it being played on the audio CD. Look through a thesaurus and select a word that has many synonyms. Then put the children into pairs and provide them with the word as a starting point and ask them to take it in turns to say a synonym related to that word. The one who stops first is the loser. If you take 'good' as the starting word, this is how a pair might play the game.

Example

Partner A	Partner B
Excellent	*Fine*
Great	*Super*
Splendid	*Superb*
Fantastic	

In this case, Partner A would win the game as they came up with more words.

Alternatively, you could give the children a time limit of one minute and see who can write the longest list of synonyms for a word in each pair.

> 💡 **TIP:** Make big posters of synonyms for common words and make sure that these are also in children's writing journals. Use these to play sentence games as well as in shared writing, and insist on them using the word banks in their own writing, choosing carefully to create a shade of meaning.

Variations
- It is also worth playing this game with common words that children use and need to vary in their own writing, e.g. *looked* and *said*. Here are some synonyms for these.

    - Looked = *examined, eyed, gaped at, gawped at, gazed, glanced, glared, glimpsed, goggled, inspected, observed, peeked, peeped, peered, regarded, scanned, scrutinized, saw, skimmed, squinted, stared, studied, surveyed, noted, viewed, watched.*

- Said = *answered, announced, asserted, babbled, bawled, chatted, cried, commented, declared, exclaimed, gossiped, hissed, mentioned, remarked, replied, responded, suggested, stuttered, stammered, uttered, whispered.*

- Other common words that children overuse include *went, saw, got, bad, good, sad, angry, beautiful, nice* and *take.*

- When looking at children's writing, jot down words that could be made more powerful and effective if a synonym had been used. Build these into the game.

5. Word Choice – Squeezing a Word
For the whole class.

Equipment:
- a whiteboard and a whiteboard pen for you
- paper and pencils or mini whiteboards and whiteboard pens for the children

Skills Developed:
- thinking about the many layers of meaning and connections that one word produces

How to Play the Game
This game is worth playing on many occasions. Start with a word and write it on the whiteboard. As an example, let's take the word 'road'. It is worth pausing to think about all the things that happen when we put a word under the microscope. We can look at it, listen to it and then think about its meaning and its associations. Here are a few areas to focus on with the class when studying a word in this way. In each case, we have started from the word 'road'.

- Words that start in the same way, e.g. *roof, rascal, run, rat, rare, ruin, run,* etc.

- Words that rhyme or share the same spelling pattern, e.g. *toad, showed, sewed, code, load,* etc.

- Words that share the same vowel sound, e.g. *show, slow, grow, mow,* etc.

- Synonyms, e.g. *alley, path, motorway, street, avenue,* etc.

- Associated words, e.g. *builder, car, lorry, journey, tarmac,* etc.

- What the word means to us (beyond the standard dictionary definition), e.g. *a path from one place to another, a link, a scar across a landscape, a slaughter house for animals, car crashes,* etc.

- Specific examples of the noun, e.g. *The Broadway, South Street, North Lane,* etc.

- Memories associated with the word, e.g. *driving route 66 with my friend Hugh, having a flat tyre on the way to school, walking across England,* etc.

- How the word is used in stories, films or other art forms, e.g. *journeys feature in many quest tales, the Hodgeheg was nearly killed on one,* etc.

- Facts about the word, e.g. *Romans built straight roads, they are made of tarmac, they need constant renewal due to overuse, maps show them,* etc.

Use this list as a starting point for 'squeezing' your own words and feel free to add more categories for the children to explore.

Such is the power of words that when we hear or see them, without consciously knowing, each one is loaded with other words, ideas, stories and memories. The word 'road' reminds Pie of his journey across America, the place where his father died and the thousands of hours that he has spent on motorways crossing the country. Each word is potentially a living library of connotations. As one child said to Pie, "I never knew there was so much in a word".

Variation

- Introduce 'warming up the word' books. Use these little notebooks as a place for mini brainstorms at the start of lessons. For instance, if you were about to introduce work on the evacuees, you might give them the words 'home' and 'stranger'. The children then list connotations rapidly. This tunes them into the theme that they are about to explore. One useful avenue is to collect everyday expressions, idioms and proverbs associated with a word, e.g. *I've reached a crossroads in my life; our paths met; it's been a long road,* etc.

6. Word Choice – The Powerful Verb Game 📷

For the whole class.

Equipment:
- a whiteboard and a whiteboard pen for you
- paper and pencils or mini whiteboards and whiteboard pens for the children
- the image CD and an interactive whiteboard (for the Variation)

Skills Developed:
- selecting powerful and effective verbs

How to Play the Game
You just cannot play this simple game too often. It is a direct and immediate way of polishing up children's writing.

Write up a number of sentences on the whiteboard. Here are some examples to get you started, but feel free to add to this.

- *The elephant went into the supermarket.*
- *The old lady went across the road.*
- *The starving man ate the meal.*
- *The Queen ate the doughnut.*
- *The chimp got hold of the clown's nose.*
- *"Get out!" he said.*
- *"Run?" she said, getting the suitcase.*
- *The thief looked through the jeweller's window.*

The children then have to identify the weak verbs and replace them with more powerful ones, e.g. *The elephant went into the supermarket* could become, *The elephant stomped into the supermarket.* Hold brief discussions about the meaning and effect that different choices make. For example, how does it alter the meaning if an elephant *trudges* or *break-dances* or *tiptoes*? Writers select words to create effects. Good writing is a matter of thinking about the effect that the word choices make – not just chucking in what someone else has decided is a 'fantastic' word.

Variations
- Carry out the same game, but ask the class to change the nouns or adverbs.

- Use an image from the CD and create sentences with powerful verbs.

7. Word Choice – The Adjective Race 📷

For the whole class.

Equipment:

- a whiteboard and a whiteboard pen for you
- paper and pencils or mini whiteboards and whiteboard pens for the children
- a timer
- the image CD and an interactive whiteboard (for the Variation)

Skills Developed:

- the ability to generate adjectives rapidly

How to Play the Game

Write up a noun on the whiteboard and give the children one minute to list as many adjectives that describe that word as possible. It is easiest for the children if you write the chosen words in this fashion, leaving a space for the adjective.

The_____dog.

The winner is the child who manages to come up with the longest list.

Example

Here are the adjectives we generated in one minute to describe the word 'dog'.

Fat
Small
Large
Skinny
Slim
Slender
Stout
Bold
Brave
Cunning
Sly
Shy
Peaceful
Desperate
Shabby
Shaggy
Calm
Quiet
Awful
Smelly
Disgraceful
Deliberate
Dirty
Dutiful

Faithful
Kind
Gentle
Angry
Savage
Snarling
Barking
Yapping
Growling
Unkempt
Generous

If you look at our list, you will notice that most of our adjectives could be used to refer to a person or some other animal – only a few are particular to the word 'dog'. This is fine as it rehearses the skill of rapidly generating possibilities.

Here are some other alternatives to the noun 'dog' that you could use for children to build their adjective lists: *cat, thief, princess, king, snake, spider, tree, ocean, mountain, tower, mirror, blanket, hat, lion, tiger*, etc.

Variation

- Use an image from the CD and ask children to list adjectives rapidly to describe it.

8. Word Choice – Name It

For the whole class.

Equipment:

- a whiteboard and a whiteboard pen for you
- paper and pencils or mini whiteboards and whiteboard pens for the children

Skills Developed:

- selecting a precise noun

How to Play the Game

This game is another key writing game that involves selecting the right word. Children tend to select nouns that are bland. For example, they might write:

he got into the car...

rather than:

he clambered into the Land Rover...

As soon as you particularise the noun (name it) then it comes alive. If the writer chooses the word 'bird', then it is of no consequence. However, an *ostrich* or *eagle* might well be.

Provide the class with sentences or a paragraph in which there are a number of bland nouns that they can particularise by 'naming' them. Here are some sentences you could use.

- *The man got into the car cautiously.*
- *The woman picked up the fruit greedily and ate it.*
- *The teacher looked at the vegetable nervously.*
- *The girl helped herself to a sweet without thinking.*
- *The dog eyed the cat savagely.*
- *A bird sat on the boy's shoulder while he picked up the thingy reluctantly.*

Look how much more interesting the sentences become when you name the noun.

- *Mr. Steady got into the Volvo cautiously.*
- *Mrs. Hungry picked up the strawberries greedily and ate them.*
- *Miss. Timid looked at the turnip nervously.*
- *Miss. Dreamy helped herself to a marshmallow without thinking.*
- *The Rotweiler eyed the kitten savagely.*
- *The parrot sat on James's shoulder while he picked up the worm reluctantly.*

When you carry out this activity with the children, remind them to change words like 'man' into a name, e.g. *Mr. Steady*, as we have done in the examples. Ask some children to read out their new sentences to the rest of the class. Discuss the impact of the adverbs in the original sentences. How did they affect the choice of noun?

<u>Extension Activities</u>

- Children can develop their new sentences a stage further by changing the verbs. We have used clues from the adverbs to make the verbs more specific in the following sentences.

  - *Mr. Steady <u>crept</u> into the Volvo cautiously.*
  - *Mrs. Hungry <u>snatched</u> the bowl of strawberries greedily and ate them.*
  - *Miss. Timid <u>eyed</u> the turnip nervously.*
  - *Miss. Dreamy <u>grabbed</u> a marshmallow without thinking.*
  - *The Rotweiler <u>glared</u> at the kitten savagely.*
  - *The parrot <u>perched</u> on James's shoulder while he picked up the worm reluctantly.*

- They could also drop in adjectives to describe the nouns and to make their writing even more exciting.

  - *Mr. Steady crept into the <u>rusty</u> Volvo cautiously.*
  - *Mrs. Hungry snatched the <u>giant</u> bowl of strawberries greedily and ate them.*
  - *Miss. Timid eyed the <u>knobbly</u> turnip nervously.*
  - *Miss. Dreamy grabbed a <u>soft</u> marshmallow without thinking.*
  - *The Rotweiler glared at the <u>quivering</u> kitten savagely.*
  - *The parrot perched on James's shoulder while he picked up the <u>wiggly</u> worm reluctantly.*

9. Word Choice – The Curious Shop 📷

For the whole class.

Equipment:
- the photocopiable page **(Prepositional Phrases)**
- paper and pencils or mini whiteboards and whiteboard pens for the children
- access to the internet
- the image CD and an interactive whiteboard (for the Variation)

Skills Developed:
- using prepositions to add extra description to a piece of writing

How to Play the Game

This simple game is very useful for helping children to add detail to their writing by using prepositional phrases. Give the children copies of the photocopiable sheet **(Prepositional Phrases)** on the next page to help them create ideas. Firstly, ask the class to think of a shop. We have found that a wizard's store works well, but that may be because of Harry Potter's influence! Then ask them to rapidly make a list of the sorts of things that might be purchased in the shop, e.g. *broomsticks, potions, spells, books, wands, jars of ingredients, invisibility cloaks, magic keys, toads, cats, hats*, etc.

Next, using the prepositional phrases, they can build a description of the store.

Examples
- **On top of the shelf…***was a row of coloured jars with what looked like stones inside them, but one blinked and Harriet realised that it was a toad.*

- **Hanging from the ceiling…***was a rusty lamp that shone a green light.*

- **On the counter…***was a white cat with startling blue eyes which was for sale.*

Collect words which help extend the description, e.g. *with, that, which.*

Variations
- Experiment with other places to use as a basis to build descriptions, e.g. *a room in a palace, a kitchen, a classroom, a cave, a deserted factory, a mad professor's lab*. You could find an image on the internet of your chosen setting and show this to the children to trigger their imaginations.

- Use prepositions to describe a setting from the CD image bank.

Prepositional Phrases

Creating a Room

On top of the shelf...

Hanging from the ceiling...

On the counter...

Under the table...

Beside the chair...

Next to the door...

Beneath the window...

Against the wall...

Creating a Landscape

In the distance...

On the hill...

Beside the lake...

Under the trees...

By the wall...

Inside the building...

From the tower...

10. Fantastic Fragments – Making Sentences

For the whole class.

Equipment:

- fiction, non-fiction and poetry books
- a whiteboard and a whiteboard pen for you
- paper and pencils or mini whiteboards and whiteboard pens for the children

Skills Developed:

- noticing imaginative word combinations

How to Play the Game

Sometimes we invent games that come from a title. This game came about just like that. Pie was thinking of games to stimulate the imagination when the idea of *Fantastic Fragments* leapt into his mind. Now, the brain sometimes does that. Without any noticeable thought processes, the brain throws up – sometimes uninvited – an idea. It is almost as if there is part of the brain busily working away and sometimes it generates insights and ideas that are useful to us. We have often found that if we want to solve a writing problem then we put it to one side, busy ourselves with something else like washing up or going for a walk or taking a nap, then when we are least expecting it and have forgotten the original problem, the answer leaps into our minds!

Anyway, to play this game, pile books onto the children's tables. It is good to include poetry and fiction, as well as some non-fiction. The children should then flick through the books to select words and fragments of sentences. Similes and metaphors are handy. They should choose unusual sounding pieces. Collect their ideas and write a selection on the whiteboard. Halves of sentences can be listed and then randomly selected and pushed together. Often these fragments can create new sentences that are nonsensical, but maybe also have a ring of weird truth about them. Here are some fragments that we have found from some of Pie's stories:

The King seized	*The grasses hissed*
How sweet	*Secret ingredient*
The feather did not move	*Stopping by the*
The tiniest of	*As the warm sun*

With a little linguistic engineering, we could now make some new sentences.

Examples

- *Stopping by the tiniest of bookshelves, the King seized the secret ingredient.*
- *As the warm sun shone, the feather did not move but the grasses hissed.*

11. The Wizard's Suitcase – Making Sentences 💿

For the whole class or the whole class organised into pairs or groups.

Equipment:

- the audio CD and a CD player
- a whiteboard and a whiteboard pen for you
- paper and pencils or mini whiteboards and whiteboard pens for the children
- a timer (for the Variation)

Skills Developed:

- generation of new ideas
- problem solving creatively

How to Play the Game

Listen to the game being played on the CD with the class. Every child loves this little game. It is simple enough to play, but often generates all sorts of ideas. All the children have to do is list what might be found inside a wizard's suitcase, *e.g. In the wizard's suitcase, I found a never-ending purse, an invisibility cloak, a lost princess's slipper...*

Try playing the game in pairs where Partner A adds in the first item, followed by Partner B, and so on. It can also be played round a circle in a group, or as a whole class. You could also vary the game by using different containers or places:

Containers	Places
Suitcase, Handbag, Rucksack, Pocket, Box, Chest, Sack, Bag, Purse, Trunk	*Den, Lair, Palace, House Laboratory, Garden shed Factory, Mind, Cottage, Office*

You could also use an alternative to the wizard. It works best if you select – or the children select – a character that has many possibilities and is well-known. This could be a fictional (Flat Stanley) or a traditional character (the Troll), but it could also be a real person, such as Henry VIII.

Example

- *In the dragon's den I found a pile of glittering treasure, a hero's severed limb, an atlas of towns to rob, a book of riddles, a poster titled 'How to capture a hobbit'...*

Variations

- Put children in pairs or small groups with a time limit – turn it into an ideas race by seeing who can write down the most ideas within a minute. The person who has written down the most suggestions is the winner.

- You could also get the children to run through the items using alphabetical order. So the first item would start with the letter 'a', the second with 'b', and so on. Here is how the whole alphabet might be used.

    In Grandma's trunk there is an antelope, a bison, a cougar, a dragon, an elephant, a ferret, a giraffe, a horse, an iguana, a jaguar, a killer bee, a lemur, a minotaur, a newt, an owl, a panther, a quail, a red fox, a sand eel, a tiger, a unicorn, a vole, a whale, an x-ray fish, a yeti and a zebra.

- It is also interesting to give categories that the items must belong to, e.g. *animals (as above), food items*, etc.

- Make the game useful to you by linking it with a subject or a story you are studying, e.g. *In the Mummy's tomb there is..., In the witch's cauldron there is...*, etc.

12. I Must Have Been Dreaming, But... – Making Sentences 💿 📷

For the whole class organised into pairs.

Equipment:

- the audio CD and a CD player
- the image CD and an interactive whiteboard
- a whiteboard and a whiteboard pen for you (if desired)

Skills Developed:

- imagining new ideas

How to Play the Game

Listen to the game being played on the CD with the children. Invite the children to invent scenarios out loud, using the starting point *I must have been dreaming, but...* Encourage them to focus on the senses to complete the phrase. To help them generate ideas about what they might have seen, heard, tasted, smelt or felt, use the magical forest image on the CD as a starting point.

Examples

- *I must have been dreaming, but I thought I **saw** Miss Jones riding on the back of a unicorn!*

- *I must have been dreaming, but I thought I **smelt** a dragon's fire.*

- *I must have been dreaming, but I thought I **tasted** the Queen's royal cup of tea.*

13. Making Sentences – The Missing Word Round

For the whole class.

Equipment:

- a whiteboard and a whiteboard pen for you
- paper and pencils or mini whiteboards and whiteboard pens for the children
- a newspaper or fiction, non-fiction, poetry books and song lyrics
- adverts and notices around the school or in magazines (for the Variation)

Skills Developed:

- considering how changing a word creates different effects

How to Play the Game

Anyone who watches the television programme *Have I Got News for You* will be familiar with the idea of *The Missing Word Round*. In the programme, the teams are presented with a newspaper or journal headline with some words blanked out. They then have to guess what might have been omitted. It is a form of cloze procedure which gives rise to all sorts of humorous suggestions.

In this class version, you could take news headlines and omit a word or two. However, there are also all sorts of other possibilities you could try with stories, non-fiction and poetry.

- Take an opening line from a story and miss out some key words.

- Try using a suspense sentence from a story with the key elements missing.

- Action sentences from the dilemma in a story would work well with children filling in the missing verbs.

- Use descriptions of characters or settings with words missing – this could be from a story book, or even from the back cover of the book.

- Try omitting some words from a heading in a chapter of a non-fiction title.

- Use an interesting line from a poem you are studying together and take out a key word.

- Take out some words from a current pop song's lyrics.

Simply write your chosen sentence up on the board and ask the children to write down the missing word.

You could play the game in a serious manner so that the children have to guess exactly what they think the author would have written, or you could play the fun version where they can be playful with their word choices. For the game to succeed, children will have to choose the right word class, as using a verb instead of a noun will not work.

Example

If the original line in an opening of a story is:

Tom stared at the cave in terror

You could write on the board:

Tom stared at the_____ in terror

Children could then try and guess what the word is and write it down:

Tom stared at the large dog in terror

Or they could come up with some playful suggestions for the missing word:

Tom stared at the frozen flames in terror
Tom stared at the banana in terror

Variation

- Split the class into groups and ask each group to collect sentences from adverts, notices around the school or in magazines or books. They should then prepare their sentences by writing them out with the key words omitted. The 'missing word' sentences can then be passed between the groups so that each group has another group's sentences. They can then work together in their groups to work out what they think is the missing word in each case.

14. Making Sentences – The Question Game 📷

For the whole class organised into pairs.

Equipment:
- the image CD and an interactive whiteboard
- a whiteboard and a whiteboard pen for you

Skills Developed:
- creating imaginative answers to questions

How to Play the Game

Many people are familiar with the game of listing questions and then swapping papers so that a partner can answer them – giving real or imaginative answers. This game was one of the ones that the surrealists used to play and has been adopted by teachers of creative writing. However, this game provides question prompts for you. Here are the key prompts which you could write up on the whiteboard for the children.

What…?
Where…?
Why…?
Who…?
How…?
When…?

You could begin by selecting a subject that everyone uses as a basis for questions, e.g. an image from the CD. In pairs, the children invent various questions, using the prompts to start each one. It can be interesting if the children pretend to ask the object the questions as if it were a person. Each pair then swaps over their questions with another pair and must come up with answers to the questions. This is most fun if the answers are impossible. For instance, if the subject was an elephant, the children might come up with:

Questions:	Answers:
What are your eyes for?	To play marbles.
Where did you get such large ears?	From a sailing ship.
Why do you walk in the sun?	To keep my mind warm.
Who helped you learn to lift tree trunks?	Superman.
Why did you find your grey skin?	I stole it from a thunder cloud.
When will you visit me?	When eternity ends.

15. Speaking – Saying Words Aloud

For the whole class.

Equipment:

- the photocopiable page **(Speaking – Clarity, Power and Expression)**

Skills Developed:

- speaking clearly and with confidence

How to Play the Game

These exercises are great fun and intended to warm-up the mouth, tongue and lips – exercising the muscles and making children more aware of the sounds they can make. Give the children a copy of the photocopiable sheet **(Speaking – Clarity, Power and Expression)** on the next page to stick in their writing journals and refer to when needed.

The mouth

Begin by getting the children to open their mouths wide like a lion yawning, then tightening them up like a disapproving aunt and finally making a large, wide grin like a laughing jester. Repeat this ten times.

Now ask the children to pretend that they are at the doctor's surgery and open their mouths wide saying *Ahhhh*, then shrivel them tight and say *Oooh!* Repeat ten times.

Next invite the children to give a long slow yawn, feeling the way their mouths open wide and their throats stretch. Ask them if they can try and yawn with their mouths closed – it's harder than it looks, but excellent for stretching the throat! Repeat ten times.

The children can then pretend they have a sticky toffee stuck in their mouths. They have to chew and chew it, poking it with their tongue to try and 'remove' it.

The tongue

Once their mouths are warmed up, it's time for the children to exercise their tongues. Ask the class to use their tongues to push their left and then their right cheeks ten times each. Then they can waggle their tongues up and down, and side-to-side making a funny noise. Now get them to try this in their mouths silently. Can they feel the tops and bottoms of their mouths? Ask them to run their tongues along their teeth, as if cleaning their teeth with their tongue!

Next, invite the class to move their tongues round and round in their mouths, first one way and then the other, like a wheel spinning and then to stick the tongue in and

out rapidly ten times. See who can curl their tongues. The children who can do this can then blow through the tunnel they create.

The lips

Now exercise the lips. Get the children to do five short kisses then five big kisses in an exaggerated way. Keeping their lips pushed out ask them to say *Oooh* and as they pull them back in to say *Eeee* like a mouse. Repeat ten times. Then ask them to blow through their lips like a horse!

Once they have warmed up their lips, you can move on to talking, by practising saying vowel sounds with the class. These often disappear in unclear speech. Repeat each vowel aloud in a chant as a class, annunciating each one as clearly as possible: *a – e – i – o – u*. Then get the children saying the vowels rapidly like machine gun fire, followed by stretching the vowels out, e.g. saying the long *ay, ee, igh, ow* and *oo* sounds.

Chant the five vowels in a musical, rhythmic sound: *aeiou, aeiou, aeiou, aeiou, aeiou*, etc. It helps if the children add hand actions for each vowel as this makes the vowels more memorable. Now try this little routine as a class chanting together:

> *T – T – T – T – T – Tay*
> *T – T – T – T – T – Tea*
> *T – T – T – T – T – Tie*
> *T – T – T – T – T – Toe*
> *T – T – T – T – T – Two*
> *M – M – M – M – M – May*
> *M – M – M – M – M – Me*
> *M – M – M – M – M – My*
> *M – M – M – M – M – Mow*
> *M – M – M – M – M – Moo*
> *N – N – N – N – N – Neigh*
> *N – N – N – N – N – Knee*
> *N – N – N – N – N – Nigh*
> *N – N – N – N – N – No*
> *N – N – N – N – N – New*

Try repeating this with other letters, e.g. *b, d, s, f, l* and *r*.

Variation

- Organise class poetry readings and performances. Use the photocopiable sheet **(Speaking – Clarity, Power and Expression)** to guide the children when thinking about how to talk with clarity, power and expression to a wide audience.

Speaking – Clarity, Power and Expression

Vary how you use your voice to change the effect you have on the audience. Think about the meaning of the words you are saying and how to convey that meaning to your audience.

Volume	Which parts should be loud and which should be spoken softly?
Speed	Fast or slow?
Pitch	Lower your voice or make it higher for dramatic effect?
Pauses	A pause can emphasise a point or create drama.
Projection	Project your voice so that everyone can hear you.
Clarity	The words need to be spoken clearly otherwise people who do not know you may find it hard to understand what you are saying.
Stress	This means where you place the emphasis when you speak. For instance, "I hoped Gran would give me a present" could be said in different ways with the stress on I, hoped, would, give, me, Gran or present.

16. Speaking – Tongue Twisters

For the whole class.

Equipment:
- the photocopiable page **(Tongue Twisters)**
- a whiteboard and a whiteboard pen for you (for the Variation)

Skills Developed:
- saying words clearly with good pronunciation

How to Play the Game

Give the children a copy of the photocopiable sheet **(Tongue Twisters)** on the next page and begin to chant some of the phrases together. Start slowly and rhythmically, encouraging the children to say the words with clarity, before building up to saying them faster.

Variation
- Vary the game and improve children's ability to write alliteratively, by working together to create highly alliterative sentences, e.g. *The dull dog dug a deep ditch desperately.*

Tongue Twisters

- *The Leith police have greasy teeth.*

- *Unique New York.*

- *Around the ragged rocks, the ragged rascal ran.*

- *A proper cup of coffee from a proper copper coffee pot.*

- *Red leather, yellow leather.*

- *Red lorry, yellow lorry.*

- *Sister Susie's sewing shirts for soldiers.*

- *She sells sea shells on the sea shore.*

- *Mixed biscuits.*

- *What noise annoys a noisy oyster? A noisy noise annoys a noisy oyster.*

- *She was a thistle sifter and sifted thistles through a thistle sieve.*

- *How much oil can a gumboil boil, if a gumboil can boil oil?*

- *How much wood could a woodchuck chuck, if a woodchuck could chuck wood?*

- *Three grey geese in a green field grazing.*

- *A stewed sow's snout.*

- *How many cookies could a good cook cook, if a good cook could cook cookies?*

- *Peter Piper picked a peck of pickled pepper. If Peter Piper picked a peck of pickled pepper then where's the peck of pickled pepper Peter Piper picked?*

17. Working Together – The Moving Mirror Game

For the whole class organised into pairs.

Equipment:
- none needed

Skills Developed:
- concentration
- imitation
- performing with expression

How to Play the Game

This game is worth playing on many occasions. Put the children into pairs. They need to be facing each other – either seated on the ground, sat on seats or standing. It's preferable if they stand as then they can use their whole bodies – much more fun!

One child is Partner A, the other Partner B. They take it in turns to lead, performing mimes for each other to copy. Start by letting Partner A lead the way – with B copying exactly what A does, so they look like a mirror, with both partners doing the same thing. Give the children a body part to focus on for each mime. For example, they might start with one hand, then both, then using their whole arm, then using the head or legs and finally moving the whole body together. The children can use varying height too – so some movements are low and some are high. Encourage them to make different shapes and move at different speeds – slow, fast, jerky, fluid, etc. Make sure that they don't ignore the face and create different expressions for their partner to copy, e.g. *angry, sad, lost, lonely, happy, smug, cruel, dreaming, tired, bored, excited,* etc. Once the children have explored this for a while, observe a few pairs as a class and applaud.

Variation
- Use the game as a precursor to role-play so the pairs can begin to think about how a character feels or what sort of person they are – and therefore begin to imitate and work on developing how they might move.

18. Working Together – The Speaking Mirror Game

For the whole class organised into pairs.

Equipment:
- none needed

Skills Developed:
- concentration
- imitation
- performing with expression

How to Play the Game

This game is useful in schools where many children have English as a second language. It improves listening, concentration and understanding sentence patterns.

Put the children into pairs. They need to sit facing each other – either seated on the ground, sat on seats or standing.

One child is Partner A, the other Partner B. They take it in turns to lead, swapping roles every so often at your suggestion. Partner A starts by thinking of a word or a sentence (prompt the child with ideas if needed) and saying it aloud. Partner B has to repeat back aloud exactly what Partner A has said. Develop the game by encouraging children to say the words and sentences in a variety of ways: with different expressions (e.g. *angry, sad, happy*, etc.) or different tones and speeds (e.g. *high, low, fast, slow*, etc.). Choose some pairs to demonstrate in front of the class, encourage and applaud everyone for trying.

UNIT 2: IMITATION GAMES

Activities to deepen children's understanding of a story.

Over time, you will develop a range of activities that help children to deepen their understanding of a story you are working on with the class. Here are some tried and tested ideas for the 'imitation' stage.

- **Dressing up clothes** – put together a bank of clothes/props for each story for role-play and performing.

- **Free role-play** – provide a play area such as a bears' cave or Grandma's cottage, complete with dressing up clothes, for children to 'play at' the story.

- **Story boxes or museums** – create boxes with items related to a story you are working on. It can include images, photos, texts and objects from the story.

- **Miming scenes** – invite volunteers to mime a scene from a story. Can the others guess which scene? Children could also mime what might happen next.

- **Act the story** – this is a very effective strategy and involves you narrating the story as the children act it out.

- **Puppet theatre** – collect or make finger or stick puppets (or felt boards) relating to the story for children to use for role-play.

- **Making 'News' programmes** – invite children to act in role as news presenters and characters from a story, asking questions about a character's choices or actions, e.g. *interviewing the Billy Goats Gruff about the Troll*. Use any relevant images from the CD, e.g. *the crash, the flood or the Olympic stadium*.

- **Objects or costumes –** this involves you telling the tale of the character and then placing an object from a story in the centre of the group for them to then decide what should happen.

- **Cut up stories** – cut up a story into sections or pictures and ask the children to re-sequence the pieces and use them to retell the story.

- **The missing link** – provide a sequence of images from a story with a key section missing. Children can then draw and tell the missing section.

- **Cloze procedure** – choose a section from a story that you want to focus upon. Omit key words for the children to complete.

- **Retell and sketch** – read a section from the story and ask the children to listen carefully and rapidly sketch the scene. Follow this with *Listen and retell*.

- **Listen and retell** – now read the same section aloud and ask the children to then retell or write it down, recalling as much as possible.

- **First thoughts** – after hearing a story, ask the children to think of a word that captures their feelings, or that seems to sum up a key theme in the story. On the count of three, tell them to all say their word aloud. Collect the words and discuss the different ideas.

- **Best lines** – invite the children to select their favourite line from a story and share it with the rest of the class.

- **Riddles** – write class riddles for objects in the story.

- **Create a text** – use the story as a basis for writing other materials linked to the plot that might give further insight into a character, e.g. *a postcard sent to Jack, the diary entry of a guard from the story of Icarus or a 'Wanted' poster for the Troll*.

- **Wondering** – as a class, take each character in turn from the story and generate questions that the children would like to ask them.

- **Pause a story** – choose a key moment to stop the action and write messages with the class, advising a character or warning them. Alternatively, you could draw a map for a character on a journey, or why not provide the old lady with a gingerbread recipe?

- **Character blog** – create a blog for a main character in the story you are working on.

1. Ping Pong Tales 💿

For the whole class organised into pairs.

Equipment:
- the audio CD and a CD player
- a story that the class knows well
- a microphone prop (for the Variation)
- a story map or story mountain (for the Variation)

Skills Developed:
- learning a story together

How to Play the Game

Introduce the children to the game by listening to it being played on the CD. Start by putting the children into pairs, facing each other. The game begins quite simply. The children take it in turns to say a word from a story they know, gradually building the complete story. For example, if Partner A says *Once* then Partner B replies *upon* to which A replies *a* and B replies *time,* and so on until the end of the tale.

The next stage is to retell a story 'bit-by-bit' or 'chunk-by-chunk'. Older children can try doing this in sentences. It can help reinforce punctuation if the children walk to the story, taking a punchy step to demarcate each sentence.

Variations
- Have pairs come out and perform for the class. Make sure everyone is cheered for being brave enough to have a go. If some children are shy, perhaps you can act as one half of the pair.

  Try putting pairs together so that the children are in a group of four. Then each pair can perform for the other pair.

- Vary the game in these ways:

  - babble gabble – talking the text rapidly
  - miming it by mouthing the words and doing actions
  - saying it like a robot or Dalek
  - have one child in the pair speaking it very fast and the other speaking it very slowly
  - have one child in the pair saying it loudly and the other softly

- You could make the game competitive by seating the class in a circle and using a microphone. The person with the microphone speaks as much of the story as they remember, before they pass it on to the person sat next to them. Continue around the circle until the whole story is told. The winner is the person who has held on to the microphone for the longest amount of time and remembered the most of the story. If you don't make it all the way round the circle, start the game again, from the person whose turn it is.

- This strategy for learning the story is a really useful way of focusing on an aspect of narrative – or non-fiction or poetry. It helps children listen carefully to patterns and then internalise them and is therefore ideal preparation for a focused writing session. You could use it to prepare for many aspects of writing, e.g.

Fiction	Non-Fiction
Suspense	Introduction to a discussion
Action	Technical description
Atmospheric setting	Reasons for an argument
Characterisation	Persuasive paragraph
Exciting opening	Formal introduction
Ending that shows how a character has changed	Explanation of how something works

Let us say that you were leading into a session on 'suspense' writing. Begin by reading a piece of suspense writing from the class novel, e.g. *an exciting paragraph from an Anthony Horowitz novel*. The children have to listen carefully and then in pairs retell that 'chunk' of the story. They can do this by learning the section together and speaking it at the same time, or by pinging a word or a sentence back and forth. It is not important that they remember the text word-for-word, they should be focusing on trying to recreate the event and capturing the atmosphere. Story mountains and maps are very handy as they provide reminders of basic patterns.

2. Freeze Frame
For the whole class organised into groups.

Equipment:
- a story that the class knows well
- a digital camera
- a whiteboard and a whiteboard pen for you (for the Variation)

Skills Developed:
- deepening understanding of sections of a story, the characters and their personalities
- visualising a story in the imagination and through body memory

How to Play the Game
Organise the class into groups and choose a section of the story to focus on. Ask each group to make a 'frozen picture' of that section of the story, using their body. Each child should represent a different character in the story. You might wish to use costume and props, if this helps. Take photos of the freeze frames so you can revisit them later.

Each character can then perform a monologue focusing on one or more of the following.

- *What has happened?*
- *What might happen next?*
- *What are they thinking/feeling?*
- *Do they have hopes or regrets?*
- *What are they about to say or do?*

Variations
- Let the children decide on the section of the story to freeze frame. Groups can secretly choose their sections and show their 'frozen pictures' to the rest of the class who must guess which part of the story they are representing, and who the characters are.

- You could try and reproduce the whole story in freeze frames with groups of children taking different sections – the beginning, the inciting incident, the middle, the crisis point, the resolution and the ending.

Use these questions to probe the characters at each point.

- *What can you see?*
- *What can you hear?*
- *What are you thinking?*
- *What has just happened?*
- *What would you like to happen next?*
- *What do you think is going to happen?*
- *What should you say?*
- *How are you feeling?*

- Ask the class to describe what they see in the freeze frames. For example, *Ronan's hand is like a curled crab, twisted around the stick. His eyes look fierce as he looms over the Princess*. Write descriptive poetry or prose to accompany the scene.

Extension Activity
- You can extend this idea, by using the images the children create with their bodies as a springboard for art projects surrounding the story, e.g. *a drawing of the scene*.

3. I Can See...

For the whole class.

Equipment:
- the audio CD and a CD player
- a story that the class knows well
- a whiteboard and a whiteboard pen for you
- paper and pencils or mini whiteboards and whiteboard pens for the children
- the image CD and an interactive whiteboard (for the Variation)

Skills Developed:
- imagining and developing the different settings in a known story

How to Play the Game
This game places the children in the story – they imaginatively engage and develop a setting from a story you are working on and consider how the characters feel and think. It can really help them take a story to heart, deepening their understanding. It is almost as if they become characters in the story, inhabiting its world imaginatively.

Tune the children into this game by listening to it being played on the CD. Pause a story that you are working on at any key point. Ask the children to discuss, draw, make notes or share ideas to describe what they can see.

Variations
- Invite children to perform a monologue to reveal their feelings and ideas. To turn this idea into a list poem, we find it works well if you use these phrases:

I can see...	*I am thinking...*
I can hear...	*I feel that...*
I can feel...	*I hope that...*
I am wondering whether...	*I regret...*
	I wish that...

- Use evocative settings from the image CD as a basis for children to list what they can see.

4. Hot-seat

For the whole class.

Equipment:

- a story that the class knows well
- a chair
- costumes and props relating to the story

Skills Developed:

- a deeper understanding of character
- speaking aloud in character
- improvisation

How to Play the Game

Set up a special chair somewhere in the classroom which is to be the 'hot-seat'. Ask a child to sit on it and pretend to be a character from the story you are working on (it might be helpful to model this first). Encourage the children to become the different characters, by using costume and props. This will give them extra confidence and be more fun! Then, the whole class can ask the person on the hot-seat questions.

Example

You are hot-seating Snow White.

Class: What's your name?
Snow White: Snow White.
Class: Why is that your name?
Snow White: Because I have skin as white as snow.
Class: Where do you live?
Snow White: In a house, in the woods.

This is a great game for testing how well a class knows the characters in the story.

 TIP: You may want to play this game in pairs if the children are shy. In this case, one child interviews the other who is in the hot seat.

Variations

- Swap the character in the hot-seat!

- You can also hot-seat new characters that are not in the story, but related to it. For example, you could hot-seat the Troll's mother, if you were studying *The Three Billy Goats Gruff.*

5. News Reporter

For the whole class organised into groups.

Equipment:

- a story that the class knows well
- a digital camera or an iPad to record the action and/or take photos
- writing journals and pencils for the children (for the Extension Activity)
- access to computers and the internet for the children (for the Extension Activity)
- local news clippings (for the Extension Activity)

Skills Developed:

- understanding different parts of the plot
- considering the story from alternative viewpoints
- journalistic recount writing

How to Play the Game

Take a story that the class knows really well and choose an important moment in that story – the 'crisis' point is probably the best. Split the children into groups (your choice of how many children in each group, depending on the class size). In the group, choose someone to be the 'news reporter' and the other people to be witnesses, or characters from the story. Then, ask the group to create a small news report scene based around that part of the story.

Example

If your story is the *Three Little Pigs* and you take your crisis point to be the wolf blowing down the second house made of wood, your news report might run as follows.

News Reporter: This is James Journo, I'm reporting for BBC Story News. I'm here today outside number two, Wood Lane following a reported disturbance. I have with me Mr. Pig who was there at the scene of the crime. Mr. Pig, tell me, what happened?

Mr. Pig: It was scary. I was in my house. All I could hear was a big 'whooshing' sound and it became very windy, like a hurricane! Then I heard a shout "I'll huff and I'll puff and I'll blow your house down!" It was a wolf outside!

News Reporter: I have here Mr. Sheep, who lives across the road. Mr. Sheep, can you confirm this report? Was it a wolf?

Mr. Sheep: It certainly was. Black as the night, with red glinting eyes. I saw it blow and blow Mr. Pig's house until the foundations started to collapse.

And so on...

Encourage the groups to improvise and rehearse the mini scenes and then show them to the class. Use a digital camera or an iPad to film the action and then view the reports.

Make sure every child has a chance to play the news reporter, if they want. Encourage them to swap roles or work in new groups on different parts of the story, so that they become very familiar with the characters and plot.

Variations

- You could be in role as the news editor and give instructions – perhaps another story breaks and some children are needed to work on a new story about another fictional incident.

- Role-play a news broadcast for other classes or in assembly.

Extension Activity

- The children could write down the action from the role-play as a news report. Give the children a range of local news clippings to magpie possible words, phrases and expressions that might be useful when writing up a news report. Use a digital camera to take images that could be used in the news report. Ideally, photograph the children dressed as characters and in role. Put the news stories onto the class blog. If possible use 'coveritlive.com' to interview a real journalist.

6. Gossiping Over the Gate ⊘

For the whole class organised into pairs or groups.

Equipment:

- the audio CD and a CD player
- a story that the class knows well

Skills Developed:

- imagining and deepening understanding of events, characters and motives in a story

How to Play the Game

Begin by listening to the game being played on the CD with the class. Children might also find it helpful if you model the idea with another teacher or Teaching Assistant before they have a go themselves.

Tell a story that the class knows well and stop the events at a key moment, or at a point when something has happened that needs some thought or discussion. Arrange the children into pairs or small groups and ask them to work in role as bystanders to the events and discuss what is happening. They could be relatives, friends, neighbours or acquaintances of the main character from the story. They should lean over an invisible gate and begin to gossip about what is happening, offering their opinions and summarising what they make of it all.

Variations

- Another way of tackling this is to play the game in pairs with one of the children in role as a minor character from the story and the other as someone not in the story. This means that the character in role will have witnessed some events and possibly be privy to more information than some random passer-by.

- Try starting a story with you and another teacher in role as two characters gossiping about what is going on in a story. This could be done as part of an assembly – then lead into telling the story itself. Recently in a school Pie witnessed an assembly being treated to a visit from a spaceman and an alien who were both characters in a story that the whole school was going to work on that week.

7. Phone a Friend 💿

For the whole class organised into pairs.

Equipment:

- the audio CD and a CD player
- a story that the class knows well
- two prop telephones (if available)

Skills Developed:

- deepening understanding of a specific character and plot
- playing in role as a character
- thinking about the world surrounding a story

How to Play the Game

This game works well if used at various key junctions in stories when characters have choices to make or are challenged by some sort of problem.

Play the track from the CD to the class to introduce the idea to them. You may also need to demonstrate this game with a Teaching Assistant, and partner less confident children when they have a go themselves.

Organise the class into pairs and pick a character and event from a story you are working on. One child should be the character from the story and the other child should be someone else in their life outside the story, e.g. *a friend, mother, grandmother, a doctor, the local shopkeeper,* etc. They might just gossip about events or alternatively one might be in role as a character that is facing a dilemma and be phoning a friend for advice, e.g. *the Large Billy Goat might phone a friend asking for advice about how to get across the bridge and escape the Troll.* It works well if you sit the children back-to-back when doing this activity, so that they can't see each other like a real phone call.

Once children have practised their conversations, invite volunteers to come to the front of the class and perform their phone calls for the rest of the class, using prop phones if you have them available.

Example

This focuses on *Jack and the Beanstalk* and is a conversation between Jack's mother and her best friend.

Jack's Mum: Hi, Amy, only me, Jack's mum, just ringing for a good old chat.

Amy next door: Hello there! How are things over your way?

Jack's Mum: Not good, you know. I thought things were improving but that's not the case.

Amy next door: Whatever has happened? It's not that naughty Jack again, is it?

Jack's Mum: I'm afraid it is. You'll never guess what he's done this time. I gave him Daisy, our prize cow, to take to the market and sell. We need the money. I've got a hole in the roof that needs repairing. Anyway, off he went to market with darling Daisy, whom I'd grown quite fond of. And you know what he comes back with?

Amy next door: Lots of gold coins I hope?

Jack's Mum: FIVE BEANS!

Amy next door: He never!

And so on...

Variations

- Pick a dilemma from a story and ask one child to play the character facing the problem and get them to decide with their partner who they need to phone in order to help them. Their partner should then play this character and they should role-play the telephone conversation they might have. This makes it rather like the famous TV show, *Who Wants to be a Millionaire* where the contestants can choose who to phone when stuck on a question. For example, *Cinderella might decide to phone up a coach hire company or a dressmaker and Jack might need to phone for lessons in playing magical harps.*

- Arrange for one child in each pair to act in role as a character. The other child should then ring the character, but not reveal who they are. The first child needs to work out who is phoning and why.

Extension Activity

- You can continue to play with this game as you progress through the story. For example, continuing from the story above, *Jack's mother could have other phone calls later in the plot when Jack's beanstalk has grown, and then when he brings back things from the giant.*

8. Agony Aunt/Uncle

For the whole class organised into pairs.

Equipment:
- the audio CD and a CD player
- a story that the class knows well
- a whiteboard and a whiteboard pen for you
- Agony Aunt columns suitable for the children to look at
- writing journals and pencils for the children (for the Extension Activity)

Skills Developed:
- thinking about a story from the viewpoint of different characters, leading to the possible invention of new characters

How to Play the Game

This game is very handy for exploring dilemmas that characters face in a story. Like so many of these games, the children may find it hard to invent spontaneously at first. However, if everyone plays the game all at once, this takes some of the 'fear' out of the drama so that it can be more like an organised extension of their own play. This atmosphere may well lead to more fruitful and extended role-play. Remember that this is not performance, but educational drama.

Start by listening to the game being played on the CD with the class. Then take a story that you are working on and choose a character who has a problem. As a class, brainstorm a list of things that the character would want to say to an Agony Aunt (or Agony Uncle depending on who takes this role) and write this on the whiteboard. Then demonstrate a conversation that the character might have with the Agony Aunt or Uncle with a Teaching Assistant, before letting the children have a go themselves in pairs.

> **TIP**: It might be a good idea to read to the children some examples of 'Agony Aunt' columns... as long as the questions and answers are child-friendly and suitable!

Example
This focuses on *The Little Red Hen.*

Bull: *Dear Agony Aunt, I live on a farm and I'm SO fed up with this annoying little hen who keeps asking me to plant corn.*

Agony Aunt: *Why are you so annoyed?*

Bull: *I don't even like corn, it's bird food. I just want to munch on my grass, but she expects me to do everything around the farm. How can I get her to leave me alone?*

And so on...

Variations
- You could play the character and the whole class can be the Agony Aunt, or Uncle, taking it in turns to offer different advice.

- Children could also work in small groups, playing the roles of several characters that all have a problem. In Cinderella's family, the ugly sisters and their mother might all go and seek advice.

- You can even use non-human characters. For example, take the trees in *Little Red Riding Hood.*

  Tree: *Hi Agony Aunt, can you help me? My nerves are jittery as I've seen a wolf slinking around between my low branches who looks mean and hungry.*

  Agony Aunt: *Well that's alright, he won't want to eat you, you're a tree!*

  Tree: *I know, but there's a little girl in a red cape that comes every Friday to visit her grandmother and today's Thursday! I'm worried about her safety!*

  And so on...

Extension Activity
- Follow up the role-play with children writing in role asking for and giving advice. In pairs, children can each write letters asking for advice and then give their letter to their partners to reply to. Many papers have such advice columns and reading a few suitable examples will tune the children into the idea. If the oral role-play has happened before the writing, the children will be likely to have more ideas and be more fluent as they will have already orally rehearsed the sorts of things that they might write.

The ENORMOUS Book of Talk for Writing Games for KS2

9. Role-play

For the whole class organised into groups.

Equipment:

- a story that the class knows well
- costumes, props and a role-play area, such as the school hall

Skills Developed:

- developing understanding of a story and characters' personalities
- improving confidence in drama play

How to Play the Game

Arrange the class into groups and using a story that the children know well, choose a section of it and ask each group to re-enact the scene, with each child in each group playing a different character. If possible, create a special area in the classroom just for role-play and have costumes and props readily available to help make the class move into imaginative play more easily.

Make sure that there is no audience to the drama. Audiences create fear in many children and then the role-play becomes stilted or silly, as a child plays for a laugh.

If children are inexperienced at role-play, take them into the hall and tell the story, inviting each child to find their own space and then re-enact it on their own in parallel to the narrative. They should take on all the different roles and move silently to the story. Leave pauses for the children to extend their mimes at relevant moments.

Variations

- Perhaps different groups in the class can perform different scenes which you can then string together so that they have created a version of the whole play! The performed scenes only need to be very simple, so long as the main plot points are included.

- Re-enact a scene that is not in the story, but that must have taken place. For example, if you're studying *The Iron Man*, you could re-enact the scene which must have taken place when Hogarth returns home, having seen *The Iron Man*.

- Pause a role-play and take out or bring in new characters. Change directions by having a phone ring, a letter arrive or someone knock at the door. Allow the participants time to freeze and then pause so that they can think what might happen next.

10. On Trial

For the whole class organised into two groups.

Equipment:

- a story that the class knows well

Skills Developed:

- exploring characters' motives and development

How to Play the Game

Choose a character from your story. Let's say we chose the Ugly Sisters from *Cinderella*. Split the class into two groups. One half is 'prosecuting', and the other half is 'defending'. Encourage the groups to come up with ideas for how they will win their court case. You can be in role as the judge or court clerk so that the whole drama can proceed along.

Begin with initial discussions between prosecutors and defenders so that arguments are laid out.

Example

Prosecutors: The Ugly Sisters are always horrible to Cinderella and that's not very fair.

Defenders: It's because they're still so upset their Mum married somebody else.

Prosecutors: The Ugly Sisters should be put in prison, they treat Cinderella like a slave.

And so on...

Follow this with a court scene, in which each side has time to lay out their arguments in total. It can help if the children use what they have learnt in discussion writing to help them structure what they will say.

> **TIP:** It is fine to deviate from the story a little – it is about building and understanding a rich background and personality for the characters and thinking about a story from different characters' viewpoints. Do the 'good' characters have a bad side too? Perhaps the Ugly Sisters caught Cinderella stealing their dresses – she is a thief too!

11. Writing in Role

For the whole class.

Equipment:
- a story that the class knows well
- a whiteboard and a whiteboard pen for you
- writing journals and pencils for the children
- old DVD boxes and art and craft materials (for the Variation)

Skills Developed:
- deepening an understanding of characters and their motives
- the ability to write different text types

How to Play the Game

Choose a character from the story you are studying in class. When you demonstrate this activity, it is best to use the main protagonist in the story. As a class, use shared writing to create a model text in role as the character. This can be a diary entry, a letter to another character, a secret message to put in a bottle, etc.

Once you have explored this as a class, the children can have a go on their own in their writing journals, perhaps picking a character of their choice. This allows children to be picking up on types of writing that have been covered in previous literacy units, e.g. *recounts, instructions,* etc.

 TIP: We have found that where writing is preceded by drama, this enhances the quality of the writing. The drama allows children to generate more ideas and begin to use language that may be helpful when writing. They also seem to be more motivated, enjoying the playful element.

Variations
- It is fun to also provide texts for a story, by writing in role. For instance, you might ask children to be in role as the Mayor and write a begging letter to the Pied Piper, persuading him to help Hamelin; Goldilocks might write a letter of apology to the Three Bears and Harry Potter might keep a diary.

- Collect some old DVD boxes for the children. Ideally, you need one for every child. This can be their 'story box'. They can design and insert a cover, put a story map and a written version of the story inside (once they know a story well, ask them to write it down, concentrating on perfect punctuation), along with other texts related to the story, e.g. *a diary entry, a letter, a log book, an email or text from a character, a map, a newspaper story,* etc.

UNIT 3: INNOVATION GAMES

Activities to deepen children's understanding of a story.

Over time, you will develop a range of activities that help children to generate and develop ideas to create a new version of a well-known tale. It is worth working on stories section-by-section. Nearly always, changes start with altering a previously created story map (see *Working with Maps* on page 38 for more on this) before telling – however, it can help to retell and just see where it takes you. Here are some common activities that you can do with the children at the 'innovation' stage.

- **Triggers** – provide a range of toys and figures for children to select from and then include in their innovated version of the main story.

- **Picture prompts** – use an image from the CD and discuss how the character, setting or event might be used within the main tale to alter the plot slightly.

- **Word banks** – this is essential for many children, especially if they have a limited vocabulary. Use firsthand experience (objects or location writing) or images from the CD as a focus for generating language banks in a rapid brainstorm.

- **Description** – create banks of language and ideas to help children create new settings, characters or events.

- **Characters** – list ideas for different character names and types but also use images to generate descriptive ideas, similes, adjectives and verbs to help build characterisation. Encourage the children to think about expressions that their new characters might say and get them to role-play conversations.

- **Openers** – discuss and list different angles for opening a story. Skim through books and collect different strategies.

- **Endings** – discuss how a story might have an alternative ending. List ideas and test some out by retelling or using shared writing.

- **Suspense and action** – use images or locations or darken a room and light a candle to generate language for suspense. Create a chase scene in the hall or playground (with 'no touch' rules) and then rapidly generate language.

- **Dialogue** – develop scenes by using mime and then write the accompanying dialogue.

- **Backtracking** – use a map to backtrack from the key dilemma and change the events leading up to the crisis. Discuss what might happen if the characters took a different route or a different sequence of events occurred. How might this alter the events and crisis?

- **Tell the changes** – instead of starting the innovation by changing the story map, challenge the children to make changes to the main story as they are retelling it. You could introduce an object or image for them to include to adapt the story.

- **Atmosphere** – try playing music as children retell the story to create a different mood.

- **Role-play a change** – begin by asking the children to enact the opening scene of a story they know well and encourage them to move the story in a new direction by a planned 'interruption'. This could be accomplished by a knock at the door, a phone ringing or someone arriving. Alternatively, you could be in role as director and call out instructions as the role-play is happening to adapt the story, e.g. *make the characters leave the setting, do not allow the characters to leave, get the characters to go to the town,* etc.

- **Deliver a message** – write a letter or postcard and intervene as children role-play the main story and deliver it. Make sure that whatever is written will steer the story in a new direction. For instance, a letter might arrive at Jack's house to say that the local council want to chop down the beanstalk as it is blocking light to nearby cottages.

- **Shorten it** – challenge the class to rewrite a story in fifty words. When the stories are shared, see if everyone can guess the tale.

1. Working with Maps

For the whole class.

Equipment:

- a story that the class knows well
- paper for story maps for class and pupil versions (see below for some suggestions of different size options)
- coloured pens
- sticky notes

Skills Developed:

- adapting a plot visually, using icons and annotations

How to Play the Game

Story maps offer children the opportunity to innovate on a known story in a very simple way. The basic maps should first be created at the 'imitation' stage where key events and language patterns of a story you have read together are drawn onto a map to act as a powerful visual reminder of the story. Children can then use these maps to help them retell the original story.

> 💡 **TIP**: When creating story maps, it is worth considering the size and shape of the paper used. A3 allows for more space, but it can be helpful to use a zigzag book shape and split a story up by paragraph or section. Rolls of wallpaper can be a tremendous way of depicting a text in bold, moving sequentially along from left to right. These could be reduced to look like 'scrolls' for legends or fairy tales. Some teachers have even used shaped paper to reflect the story theme or type, e.g. *fairy tales drawn on paper in the shape of a castle.*

When innovating on a story, the map of the original version is often a natural starting point. Where these have been drawn lovingly as works of art, children will be reluctant to tamper with them and will need to draw a new map. However, simple sketches lend themselves to being altered. Sticky notes come in all sorts of shapes and sizes and can be used to demonstrate changing the class map, but are also useful for children to add to their own maps to alter events. We like to use sticky notes shaped like arrows as well as sticky speech bubbles for adding new dialogue.

Demonstrate to the class how to make changes to the original story by crossing out text and images, adding additional features and using sticky notes. It helps to tackle changing a story section-by-section. At first do not make too many changes or the story may fall apart – and be wary of making changes that have consequences later on! Once you have made the changes, you will have a new version of the story that can then be retold using the map as a prompt. Maps can be transposed onto flow charts or by 'boxing up' so that the pattern of the text becomes more obvious as a precursor to writing.

2. Story Partners

For the whole class organised into pairs.

Equipment:

- a story that the class knows well

Skills Developed:

- retelling a new version of a story
- making and developing changes to create different effects

How to Play the Game

Whilst many children like to make changes to a story using a story map, there are an equal number who prefer to work on the story orally. Perhaps those like to work from the map have more of an inclination to be 'planners' whilst those who like to retell first and see what happens take a more 'explorative' approach.

Model how to play this game with a Teaching Assistant. Demonstrate how you tell the story orally to your partner with subtle changes to adapt the plot, characters or dialogue. The Teaching Assistant should act as an audience as you create your new version, listening carefully, but also giving sensitive and supportive feedback. They can also ask you questions to help you generate new ideas and keep the narrative flowing. These may centre on key aspects of innovation:

- changing characters
- altering the locations
- changing the time of day
- using the weather to create a mood
- building description
- altering what is said
- changing what happens
- deciding on a new dilemma
- changing the direction of a story
- finding a new opening
- finding a new ending

It is helpful to use open ended questions as well as a phrase such as, *tell me more about…* to guide the innovator through the process.

Finally the Teaching Assistant can identify pieces in a story that worked well and make helpful suggestions about how it could be improved.

Once you have modelled this process, arrange the class in pairs so that they can have a go. Listen in on their retellings and offer help and prompts when the conversation dries up. Some children may like to share their new stories with the rest of the class.

3. Yo-Yo Tales 💿

For the whole class organised into pairs.

Equipment:

- the photocopiable page **(Yo-Yo Tales)**
- the audio CD and a CD player
- a story that the class knows well
- a large story map of the known story
- pens

Skills Developed:

- retelling a new version of a story
- making and developing changes to create different effects

How to Play the Game

This game uses the 'ping pong' technique of two people telling a story word-by-word, sentence-by-sentence or chunk-by-chunk. For example, if a pair was to tell it word-by-word, the first child would say the first word of the story, then the second child would say the second word and so on, until the story is complete.

Start by listening to the game being played on the CD. Then take the story that you have been working on and begin to innovate, making changes to the story. It can help to discuss the different aspects of a story that might be changed first. Give the children the photocopiable sheet **(Yo-Yo Tales)** on the next page to guide them through the different possibilities. Start simply, by making just a few changes.

You might then change the map together as a class and then ask the children to retell the new version in pairs, using the 'ping pong' technique. Alternatively, you could get each pair to just start telling the story using the technique and make up the changes as they go along, drawing on the photocopiable page to help them decide what changes to make.

💡 **TIP**: It is worth asking the children to only alter a few things; otherwise they may find it hard to tell the story. So – limit the changes. Ask children to work in pairs and just change the nature of a character. Then hear some examples. Then ask them to just change the setting and see what happens.

Variation
- Add in extra items that may take the tale in a new direction. These could be:

  - selected from the photocopiable page (**Story Menu**) on page 68 using a dice
  - showing the children an image that has to be included
  - putting together a selection of objects in a story chest for the children to choose from

In this way, Little Red Riding Hood might be sent travelling, clutching a mobile phone and on the way have to call at a fish and chip shop!

Yo-Yo Tales

Try changing:	Innovation ideas:
How the story begins	
Characters' names	
Characters' behaviour	
What characters say	
Characters' motives	
Settings	
Time of year or day	
Different sort of weather	
Objects or animals in the story	
Key events	
How problems come about	
How problems get solved	
How the story ends	
Try adding:	
New objects	
New problems	
New characters	

The ENORMOUS Book of Talk for Writing Games for KS2

4. Story Swapping

For the whole class organised into pairs.

Equipment:
- the audio CD and a CD player
- a story that the class knows well
- a large story map of the known story
- pens
- a bank of characters, settings and ideas (or objects to stimulate ideas)
- writing journals and pencils for the children

Skills Developed:
- creating new versions of stories by making the simplest of changes

How to Play the Game
This is innovation at its simplest. It involves the children getting to know the original story really well so that they can retell it, using a map and actions.

 TIP: Younger children and less confident older children may find it helpful to learn the original stories word-for-word. This helps them internalise sentence patterns so that they begin to become part of their linguistic repertoire.

To create new versions of the story, children can simply 'swap' different aspects of the story for alternatives. Listen to the game being played on the CD and then model how to make these simple swaps on the story maps. For example, the Gingerbread Man might become a Gingerbread Tiger and instead of meeting a cow, a horse, a dog and a cat before being eaten by a fox, the tiger might encounter a lion, an elephant, a cheetah and monkey before being eaten by a crocodile!

With very young children, only make a few changes at first. Too many can cause confusion. Keep returning to the key questions with the class – does the new version make a good story? Did we enjoy the story? Did it amuse, entertain or move us? The children should tell and retell their story in pairs until they become fluent with the new version before telling it to their group or the class. They can then write the new versions down.

 TIP: Most young children benefit from having a bank of characters, settings and ideas to choose from. These might be on cards, actual objects or a class list of suggestions

Variation
- Characters can be swapped over, but so too can settings (including the weather), creatures and objects. Children can also make changes to the descriptions, perhaps replacing adjectives or adverbs or making up new similes or metaphors.

5. Embellish

For the whole class organised into pairs.

Equipment:
- the audio CD and a CD player
- a story that the class knows well
- a large story map of the known story
- pens
- writing journals and pencils for the children

Skills Developed:
- creating new versions of stories by making simple changes
- embellishing stories to create different effects

How to Play the Game

As children gain confidence in storytelling, they will start adding and embellishing in a playful manner as a matter of course and it's up to you to encourage such additions. These might be at a fairly simple level, for instance just adding in a little description so that, *Early one morning...* becomes *Early one wintry morning...*

Listen to the game being played on the CD with the class and then model retelling a story they all know with a few significant embellishments or additional sections. It is a good idea to display the map for the original story as you tell your new version so that the children can see where you are expanding the narrative. You could then add the new material to the map, before inviting the children to have a go at the activity themselves.

Older children might take a story section-by-section and 'work on it'. This could mean:

- deepening the characterisation and developing the dialogue
- building descriptions of key objects, creatures, places and people
- embellishing settings to create a particular atmosphere
- making the opening more intriguing to hook a reader's interest
- adding extra scenes or events to build further tension
- injecting suspense by slowing a passage down
- creating a more dramatic ending

Encourage the children to spend time discussing their ideas in pairs before developing an aspect. Pick a few pairs to perform their new versions to the class. It provides a good opportunity for the class to give their feedback, explaining what worked well and making suggestions for how a section might be developed further.

> **TIP:** Sometimes in the rush to 'get some writing in the books', we as teachers miss out this aspect of developing narrative. It is worth spending time on this, working orally at first before committing ideas to paper – especially if you have children for whom writing is demanding and find it hard to create 'on the spot'. Have fun by adding silly ideas in and see what effects can be created. This often 'loosens' the imagination!

6. Alteration

For the whole class organised into pairs.

Equipment:

- the audio CD and a CD player
- a story that the class knows well
- a large story map of the known story
- pens
- writing journals and pencils for the children

Skills Developed:

- creating new versions of stories by making simple changes
- embellishing stories to create different effects

How to Play the Game

An alteration to a story is a change that has consequences that mean that other parts of the tale need changing. Listen to the game being played on the CD to introduce the idea to the children. Then take a story that the children know well and begin to make some pretty dramatic changes to the class story map. Let the children suggest what should be changed and discuss each idea. You could alter the setting, the historical period, the nature of characters, the ending or even alter the actual type of story. For instance, Pie once saw Year 5 children perform a version of *The Three Bears* as a gangster rap!

Once you have finished your alterations to the class story map, organise the class into pairs for them to have a go at changing a story. Set them specific challenges in order to make their changes. They could:

- alter the nature of the main character
- turn a scary setting into a cheerful one
- change the ending so that it is sad (or happy)
- alter the opening to make the main character sound unpleasant
- make the villain into a good character
- give the main character a mobile phone
- interrupt the story with a telephone ringing or a knock at the door
- introduce a message that is found that alters what happens next
- give the villain a lie-in on the morning of the action
- have the police arrive before the crime happens

The pairs should take the story section-by-section, discussing ideas before making the alterations. It is worth having some of the children perform their new versions, getting feedback from the class before moving into writing.

 TIP: Invite the children to make a list of ideas for alterations. They can then select from this list to make their alterations.

---

7. Changing the Genre 💿

For the whole class.

Equipment:

- the audio CD and a CD player
- a story that the class knows well
- a large story map of the known story
- a whiteboard and a whiteboard pen for you
- writing journals and pencils for the children

Skills Developed:

- transposing a tale into a different genre

How to Play the Game

This involves taking a story that all the class know already and putting it in a different genre and then changing the story so that it suits this new choice. For instance, *Little Red Riding Hood* might be retold as a space science-fiction story, e.g.

One day on the moon, Little Yellow Stardust was told by her mother to go and visit her grandmother who lived on the next planet...

Introduce the activity by listening to the game being played on the CD. Then brainstorm the different fiction genres with the children and write these on the whiteboard, e.g. *mystery, thriller, horror, detective, school, fantasy, science-fiction, historical, domestic, hospital, myth, legend, fairy tale, animal,* etc. Choose a genre from this list and help the children to become very familiar with it. For instance, if you are thinking that you might take a story and then retell it as a detective story it would be worth investing time in reading Anthony Horowitz's stories such as *The Falcon's Malteser*. Older pupils could investigate the series about the Diamond brothers, who run a detective agency. Raid books from the chosen genre for any typical turns of phrase or sentence patterns and make a class list of the typical events, characters and settings that typify the selected genre.

Write your selected story in the new genre together with the children, incorporating their suggestions, before letting them loose to have a go themselves.

Variation

- Learn the opening of a well known story, e.g. *The Three Little Pigs*. Then ask the children to choose a genre from the list and re-write just the opening in this style. They can then read their example aloud and see who can guess the genre. The person who guessed correctly should give the clues that gave it away.

8. Viewpoint 💿

For the whole class organised into groups.

Equipment:

- the audio CD and a CD player
- a story that the class knows well
- a large story map of the known story
- writing journals and pencils for the children

Skills Developed:

- creating new versions of stories by retelling what happened from a different character's point of view

How to Play the Game

This game involves taking a story that the class know really well and retelling it from a different character's viewpoint, so instead of narrating it from the main character's perspective, they might tell it from the viewpoint of a less significant character or even the baddie! It is a useful game as it helps children to see things from someone else's viewpoint and therefore helps to develop characterisation. Let the class listen to the game being played on the CD where Pie tells the story of *The Three Billy Goats Gruff* from the Troll's perspective and makes him sound good – the children might even begin to feel sorry for him!

You could then get the children to interview key characters from a story that they know well in role as TV presenters or journalists, asking the characters to explain what happened and what they thought from their perspective. To begin with, you might choose to play the part of the character being interviewed so that the children get the idea, before organising the class in groups with half the group playing characters from the story and the other half interviewing them about their actions.

Another way into this would be to role-play a character from a story coming home and chatting through what happened with a relative.

> 💡 **TIP:** Many children find it helps to draw a new story map before trying to retell what happened from another angle. We have seen wonderful examples of wolves being outraged by the behaviour of their elderly next door neighbours!

- Why not try telling the story from a different character's perspective and getting the children to act out what is happening as it is being told? This could be performed in quite a loose fashion with everyone inhabiting their own space in a hall and each child adopting a different character. When their character is not 'on scene', they should sit quietly and wait. They could then rewrite the events and reflect this different viewpoint by writing a diary entry or letter to a friend about what has just happened.

- This also works well if children write about stories as journalists and are challenged to 'take an angle'. For instance, their editor might be sympathetic towards giants and ask for an article that portrays Jack as a local thief!

9. Skeleton Stories

For the whole class.

Equipment:

- the photocopiable page (**Skeleton Stories**)
- a whiteboard and a whiteboard pen for you
- writing journals and pencils for the children
- a story that the class knows well (for the Variation)

Skills Developed:

- innovating and expanding upon a story
- retelling a story using children's own words and ideas from a simple story skeleton

How to Play the Game

Give the children the photocopiable sheet (**Skeleton Stories**) on the next page so that each child in the class has one. Demonstrate how to expand one of the skeleton stories into a fuller tale, using the same simple plot, but adding and embellishing the detail. Box up the key scenes from one of the skeleton stories into a flow chart and then embellish each of the scenes. Once you have rewritten the story, read the class both versions – the short, simple original and the extended, innovated version so that they can hear the difference. They will then learn that an interesting story has basic, skeleton plot points at its heart. Children can then have a go at these themselves, choosing their own skeleton story from the photocopiable page to work on.

Example
Skeleton Story 11: *There was a boy who lived in the countryside. One day he went for a walk. He wasn't looking where he was going and he fell down a well. Eventually, he was rescued.*

Extending the beginning of Skeleton Story 11: *Once upon a time, there was a little boy named Jamal. He lived in the house on the highest hill, in the most beautiful corner of England. Every day, he would take a walk around the hills, drinking in the sweet unpolluted air and feeling lucky to live there…*

> **TIP:** You can then make up your own skeleton stories, or ask the children in your class to make up ones for each other.

Variation
- Use a story that you have been studying in detail and try to reduce its main plot points to a fifty word story. This will really help the class understand the skeleton bones of a story and then make them realise that they can use skeleton story structures to invent fantastic ones too!

Skeleton Stories

1.

Main character breaks into a house. Destroys something and runs away.

2.

An old man has never had any luck all his life. He goes on a journey to the end of the country to find his luck. But, on the way back, he realises he passed all his luck on the way there!

3.

A girl is abducted by aliens. The girl is returned to earth.

4.

A main character buys a ring at the market. The ring gives him/her special powers. He/she use their powers to do bad things. The ring is lost.

5.

A professor invents a new talking, walking robot. But soon the robot starts to take control of everything!

6.

A main character finds a talking animal. Together they solve crime.

7.

A small girl discovers she has magical powers. She uses these powers for good and defeats an enemy.

8.

A girl goes somewhere her parents tell her she should not. She meets something/someone scary. She runs back home.

9.

An orphan is raised in the forest by animals. He is found and taken to the city to live with a human family. He doesn't adapt well to city life. He is returned to the forest and his animal family.

10.

A main character goes on a journey to try and find some lost treasure. He/she finds the treasure. He/she returns home.

11.

There was a boy who lived in the countryside. One day he went for a walk. He wasn't looking where he was going and he fell down a well. Eventually, he was rescued.

10. Using Images 📷

For the whole class.

Equipment:

- the image CD and an interactive whiteboard
- a story that the class knows well
- writing journals and pencils for the children
- access to computers to create multi-media presentations of stories (if desired)

Skills Developed:

- innovating on a known story using images

How to Play the Game

You can use images at any stage of innovation as a prompt or challenge to the children. When asked to change a setting, some children will just go blank. This may be through uncertainty or just plain fear! Very young children are often happier to innovate when given choices, such as being shown a box of animals and asked to choose a different animal to have instead of the Little Red Hen. Older pupils find using objects handy, but can also draw on images for extra inspiration.

Begin by using the images on the CD freely. These may act as a trigger or stimulus to innovation. Children might want to use a character, setting, animal, event or object and include it in their story. Of course, images might be used in a multimedia presentation of a story or to illustrate a page in the children's writing journals relating to a story that they have written.

Variation

- Challenge a group of children by asking them to retell a story that they know well as far as a key scene and then introduce a character image for them to weave into the story. You could also do this with a setting image, animal image or object image. When providing these challenges, remind the children that the content in the image could be mentioned in passing and does not have to be central to their story.

UNIT 4: INVENTION

Activities to develop children's ability to invent stories.

Here are some helpful ideas that you can do with the children at the 'invention' stage. They will help get rid of the fear of the blank page by creating the right environment for writing and giving them plenty of story triggers and starting points for their stories.

- **Plot patterns and techniques** – before children begin writing, encourage them to jot down the plot patterns they know, e.g. *warning, quest, portal,* etc. They can also make a note of the stories they enjoy that are examples of these, along with some examples of the techniques they have learnt, e.g. *suspense, action,* etc. They can then draw on all of this information when planning their own stories.

- **Story maps** – let children draw stories and retell in pairs before writing so that they have time to let the story evolve.

- **Dressing up clothes** – have a collection of costumes and accessories for children to use for improvisation activities. You could also arrange for an adult to dress up and visit the class in character for the children to interview to spark story ideas.

- **Story box** – put together a collection of objects that will help stimulate children's imaginations. Children can then choose one item or a selection of items from the box to include in their story. You could also add a new object every day or week and 'discover it' with the children. What story accompanies the object?

- **The Lion, the Witch and the Wardrobe** – challenge children to think of an animal, a character and a place and weave them into a story.

- **Buttons and shells** – you could distribute a selection of buttons or shells around the class. Children can think about what the shell is saying when they hold it to their ear, or who owned the button. Introducing objects like this can give children a starting point for their story or help to drive the narrative when they get stuck during the story.

- **Story mountain connectives** – arrange the class into groups of five and challenge each group to create a short story orally following the 'story mountain structure' so that it includes an **opening**, a **build-up**, a **problem**, a **resolution** and an **ending**. Each person in the group is responsible for one of the five sections. They should use an appropriate connective to start their section off, e.g. *Once upon a time...* at the beginning; *Unfortunately...* when the problem occurs and *Finally...* at the end. When they have told their section, they can pass the story to the next person in the group to tell their part.

- **Journey stories** – arrange the children into small groups to devise a journey story. Each person should write a different section or chapter. Journey stories are easiest when each chapter is another mini adventure on the traveller's way. You could then get each group to tell their story to the rest of the class, walking around the school and stopping at various points to tell each section. Which places have the best atmosphere for certain parts of the story?

- **Secrets, wishes, fears** – create a bank of character secrets, wishes and fears with the class. Write them out on small pieces of coloured paper – using one colour for each of the three sets of ideas. Fold them up and put them in a box. Children can then pick one from the box at random and use it as a starting point for their stories. Alternatively, they can pick three different coloured pieces of paper from the box and combine the ideas to create their stories.

- **Messages** – arrange for a message or an email to arrive for the class from a character. The message should explain the character's predicament and can be used by the children as a plot trigger.

- **Atmospheric stories** – lower the blinds, light a candle and challenge the class to write a story that starts with someone in a dark house or dungeon, lighting a candle.

- **Story trail** – create a story trail round the school. At each stopping point there might be a word, sentence, object, character or clue to collect and use in a story.

- **Enliven a story** – once children have created their main story, they can write some accompanying texts around it, e.g. *a postcard, a letter, a diary entry, an advert, a map, a text message, an email, a letter to the newspaper, a news report or bulletin, a poster, a set of instructions, a character's biography, a police log,* etc.

> The following games: *Pie and Poppy's Perhaps Game*; *101 Uses*; *How to Catch the Moon*; *How to Tame an Ogre, Where Might you Find a Fairy's Home?* and *How to Get to the Top of a Mountain* can be played orally with the whole class contributing ideas that you note down on the whiteboard. Alternatively, children may work in groups or pairs, brainstorming ideas for a set time before coming together to share ideas as a class.

1. Pie and Poppy's Perhaps Game ⊙ 📷
For the whole class or the whole class organised into pairs or groups.

Equipment:
- the audio CD and a CD player
- a whiteboard and a whiteboard pen for you
- paper and pencils or mini whiteboards and whiteboard pens for the children (if playing the game in pairs or groups)
- writing journals and pencils for the children
- the image CD and an interactive whiteboard (for the Variation)

Skills Developed:
- using familiar starting points for generating ideas

How to Play the Game
Imagining involves more than just the ability to see things in your head, it also involves playing with what you know and adapting it, making new combinations, drawing on different aspects of life to see what might happen. Stories and poems often grow in this way as the writer 'imagines', taking some sort of starting point – real or pretend – and then guiding the day-dream to find what the characters might do. It is like creating a strange journey which is guided in a knowing manner, but also allows the characters to take on a life of their own so the unexpected occurs.

This game involves children taking an ordinary character, animal or object and making something extraordinary happen, by using the word 'perhaps', e.g. *Perhaps the whiteboard writes secret messages to me.*

First of all, listen to the game being played on the CD so that the children become familiar with how it works. Then organise the class according to how you wish to play the game (pairs, groups or the whole class with individuals taking it in turns to make suggestions and you noting these down on the whiteboard). Give the class a few minutes to come up with various possibilities using the word *Perhaps* as their starting point. They may begin by using objects in the classroom to generate scenarios, but should soon be able to include people, animals and objects from their imaginations.

Examples
- *Perhaps a cat sprouts wings.*
- *Perhaps a computer can read your mind.*
- *Perhaps a new teacher arrives and you discover that he is a spy.*
- *Perhaps you catch the sofa talking to the carpet late one night.*
- *Perhaps you wake up and see all your toys running round the room.*
- *Perhaps you get stuck in a lift with a woman carrying a snake and it escapes!*

If you have played the game in pairs or groups, come together as a class at the end and share some of the scenarios because listening to other ideas will generate more thoughts. To finish the game, ask the children individually or in their pairs to select one of their 'perhaps' sentences and extend it by telling the story of what happened in full.

Variation
- Try all focusing on the same subject. Use an image from the image CD for everyone to write some 'Perhaps' ideas about.

2. 101 Uses 📷

For the whole class or the whole class organised into pairs or groups.

Equipment:
- the image CD and an interactive whiteboard (to display any of the following pictures: a boat, hats, a lantern, the moon, a car, mobile phones, a pumpkin, flip-flops, a shooting star or a teddy bear) or a selection of objects
- a range of different objects, e.g. *a mirror, a shell, a feather, a leaf, etc.*
- a whiteboard and a whiteboard pen for you
- paper and pencils or mini whiteboards and whiteboard pens for the children (if playing the game in pairs or groups)

Skills Developed:
- inventing new ideas, based on imagery, using a modal verb

How to Play the Game

This game is similar to the *Perhaps* game as it is about imagining different uses for an object that are out of the ordinary. If possible, bring in a range of different objects, e.g. *a mirror, a shell, a feather, a leaf,* etc. You don't need to do this, but having something concrete to look at helps to stimulate ideas. Alternatively, you can use the suggested images listed above from the image CD.

Then organise the class according to how you wish to play the game (pairs, groups or the whole class with individuals taking it in turns to make suggestions and you noting these down on the whiteboard). We usually begin this game with everyone putting hands up and making suggestions. At first, you may well get obvious suggestions, so for a 'mirror', children might say *use it as a light* or *use it to keep warm*. If the ideas are mundane, make a suggestion or two just to open up more playful ways it could be used.

Example
Here are some ideas for a star.

- *You could juggle with it in a circus.*
- *You could have two stars instead of eyes.*
- *You could use it as a torch at night.*
- *You could play marbles with several stars.*

3. How to Catch the Moon

For the whole class or the whole class organised into pairs or groups.

Equipment:

- a whiteboard and a whiteboard pen for you
- paper and pencils or mini whiteboards and whiteboard pens for the children (if playing the game in pairs or groups)

Skills Developed:

- the ability to generate imaginative ideas, using instructional language

How to Play the Game

This game never fails to be a hit with children and is a continuation from the previous game. Set the class the challenge of how they would catch the moon – perhaps modelling some suggestions so that they get the idea of the game. Then organise the class according to how you wish to play the game (pairs, groups or the whole class with individuals taking it in turns to make suggestions and you noting these down on the whiteboard).

Examples

- *Use a giant's lasso.*
- *Borrow Spiderman's net of spider webs.*
- *Shrink it.*
- *Eat it – it is really made of cheese.*
- *Find a mouse trap and use this as a model to build a larger version to trap the moon.*
- *Lie in wait and when it falls asleep, pounce.*
- *Leave out some bait for the moon to eat.*
- *Phone for the moon police and let them do the job.*

If you have played the game in pairs or groups, come together as a class at the end and share some of the ideas that the children came up with.

Variations

- There as many variations on this idea as there are things in the universe. Subjects that work equally well are: *the stars, the sun, a cloud, the night, the day, a comet, the milky way, a wave, a snow storm, the wind, lightning and thunder.*

- You change the challenge as follows.

  How to please...
  How to annoy...
  How to become...
  How to make...

4. How to Tame an Ogre

For the whole class or the whole class organised into pairs or groups.

Equipment:

- a whiteboard and a whiteboard pen for you
- paper and pencils or mini whiteboards and whiteboard pens for the children (if playing the game in pairs or groups)

Skills Developed:

- the ability to rapidly generate creative ideas, using imperatives

How to Play the Game

This game might be very useful for some teachers! The idea is simple enough – how might we tame an ogre? It would be handy to discuss the nature of ogres and agree on what they are like – moody, often hungry and in need of regular meals due to their enormous size, lonely, shunned by many, ferociously ugly, believed to be very stupid and slow-witted. Think of *Shrek* as a reference point!

Set a scenario – an ogre has moved into the locality and poses a threat to the community. What ideas do the children have to tame it? To get the discussion started you may need to suggest a few ideas and write these on the whiteboard so that children get the idea and feel confident enough to have a go themselves. Then organise the class according to how you wish to play the game (pairs, groups or the whole class with individuals taking it in turns to make suggestions and you noting these down on the whiteboard).

Examples

- *Advertise in the lonely hearts column for a female ogress who is interested in marriage.*
- *Tempt it with the promise of regular meals.*
- *Use shiny objects to attract it so that you can get close to him and begin to start a friendship.*
- *Sing an ogre's lullaby to soothe its temper.*
- *Offer it free accommodation under a bridge.*
- *Provide an ogre bonus scheme based on good behaviour.*
- *Offer a place at ogre school so it can learn new skills.*
- *Set up ogre television and radio stations.*
- *Set up a local ogre smoothie bar and use soothing ingredients for 'the smoothie that soothes ogres'.*
- *Give free vouchers for ogre burgers and mud milkshakes.*

If you played the game in pairs or groups, come together as a class afterwards to share some of the ideas the children came up with.

You could then extend the discussion and encourage children to think about the advantages of having a tame ogre in the community. A tame ogre that is well disposed towards its owner could be very handy. Not only would it provide good local security, but might also be able to carry out heavy duties such as lifting, carrying and fetching. Very useful to have a friendly ogre about the place, if your car breaks down leaving you stranded miles from home. A few strides and you will be transported back to safety!

Variation
- Try the same game, but with other fearsome, fairy tale or mythical creatures, e.g. *a dragon, a goblin, a hobgoblin, a sea serpent, Medusa, Minotaur,* etc.

5. Where Might you Find a Fairy's Home?

For the whole class or the whole class organised into pairs or groups.

Equipment:
- a whiteboard and a whiteboard pen for you
- paper and pencils or mini whiteboards and whiteboard pens for the children (if playing the game in pairs or groups)

Skills Developed:
- the ability to rapidly generate creative ideas around one topic, using prepositions

How to Play the Game
This is another listing game, this time considering where a fairy might set up home. First of all, it might be worth discussing ideal conditions for a fairy as a class – they are very small, shy and need camouflage. Once children are familiar with the characteristics of a fairy, organise the class according to how you wish to play the game (pairs, groups or the whole class with individuals taking it in turns to make suggestions and you noting these down on the whiteboard) and give the children a set time to think of possibilities of where a fairy may set up home.

If you played the game in pairs or groups, regroup afterwards and make a class list on the whiteboard of the children's suggestions as rapidly as possible. The more ideas that are thrown into the melting pot, the more the children create. This is because one idea so often prompts another. The ideas act as catalysts to thinking.

Examples
- *Under the bark of an oak tree.*
- *Inside a stone.*
- *Under a car bonnet.*
- *In an acorn cup.*
- *In a daffodil's throat.*
- *Under a rhubarb leaf.*
- *Under Mary Poppins' umbrella.*
- *In a pelican's beak.*

> **TIP:** You will notice that prepositions are vital to this game so it may be helpful to list some on the whiteboard: *under, in, on top of, beneath, inside, beside, near, close to, behind,* etc. Try making places 'special' by naming them. So it is not, *in a palace,* but *in King Arthur's palace.*

Variation
- Play the same game using other mythical creatures.

6. How to Get to the Top of a Mountain 📷

For the whole class or the whole class organised into pairs or groups.

Equipment:
- the image CD and an interactive whiteboard (to show a picture of a mountain) or an image of a mountain you have found on the internet
- a whiteboard and a whiteboard pen for you
- paper and pencils or mini whiteboards and whiteboard pens for the children (if playing the game in pairs or groups)

Skills Developed:
- generating new ideas
- problem solving creatively

How to Play the Game

This is another game that goes down very well. The poet Roger Stevens suggested a different version to this one, and like so many things, it has developed into our own version. That's the way with games.

The challenge is quite simple. The children have to think of as many ways as they can to get to the top of a mountain. Show the picture of the mountain from the image CD or find an alternative one on the internet.

At first, you will get all the expected answers – *climb, walk, ride a motorbike, fly in a helicopter,* etc. After a while, try making a few creative suggestions to stimulate further ideas. Then organise the class according to how you wish to play the game (pairs, groups or the whole class with individuals taking it in turns to make suggestions and you noting these down on the whiteboard).

Examples
- *Steal an eagle's wings and fly.*
- *Use a rope ladder dangling from a cloud.*
- *Find a giraffe with a very long neck.*
- *Catch a lift on a phoenix's back and fly.*
- *Borrow Perseus's winged sandals.*
- *Use the lift from Charlie and the Great Glass Elevator.*
- *Tame a flying unicorn.*
- *Hitch a lift in a hot-air balloon.*
- *Make friends with a dragon to fly up there.*
- *Jump onto an unsuspecting ogre's back and get a lift.*

If you played the game in pairs or groups, regroup afterwards and make a class list on the whiteboard of the children's suggestions.

> **TIP:** If you want to see a child and teacher friendly website, please visit Roger Stevens' site: www.poetryzone.co.uk. It is the best poetry site there is for primary schools.

Variation
- You can play many different versions of this game, e.g. *how to cross an ocean or how to cross the Grand Canyon.*

7. Mistress of Mysteries and Master of Mistakes

For the whole class organised into pairs.

Equipment:
- a whiteboard and a whiteboard pen for you
- a dictionary (if desired)
- paper and pencils or mini whiteboards and whiteboard pens for the children
- writing journals and pencils for the children

Skills Developed:
- generating new alliterative combinations

How to Play the Game

This is an easy game to play and can produce some interesting and intriguing results. The imagination is based on memory, but it is also about making new combinations and manipulating what you know to create new ideas and images.

Begin simply by making a list of nouns, verbs, adjectives and adverbs on the whiteboard that begin with the same letter – a flick through the dictionary might be helpful. As the name of the game alliterates using the letter 'm', let's start with this. Three nouns we could use are: *melody, mirror* and *mud.* Three verbs are: *menace, mimic* and *muddle.* Three adverbs are: *maybe, miserably* and *mostly.* Finally, three adjectives could be: *mean, merry* and *milky.*

Once you have your word lists, model how to add these to the end of *The Master of* or *The Mistress of* to create unusual, alliterative character names. Children can then have a go in pairs, drawing on the word lists on the whiteboard.

Examples
- *The Master of Mirrors.*
- *The Master of Melody.*
- *The Master of Mud.*
- *The Mistress of Mimicry.*
- *The Mistress of Muddling.*
- *The Mistress of Menace.*
- *The Master of Maybe.*
- *The Master of Mostly.*
- *The Master of Miserably.*
- *The Mistress of Meanness.*
- *The Mistress of Merriment.*
- *The Mistress of Milkiness.*

 TIP: You will find that some words have to be adjusted slightly so that they work.

Once children have compiled their list of characters, they could choose a favourite idea and extend it by saying what that character does, e.g. *The Mistress of Merriment leaves tickles under cushions, hides giggles in boxes and guffaws in caves...*

Variation
- Try choosing different jobs, e.g. *the clown of..., the nurse of..., the teacher of..., the builder of..., the sailor of..., the dancer of..., the footballer of..., the actor of...,* etc. These can be matched with the relevant letter of the alphabet to produce the alliterative effect.

8. The Authors of the Ridiculous

For the whole class organised into pairs.

Equipment:

- the photocopiable page **(Books Written by the Authors of the Ridiculous)**
- a whiteboard and a whiteboard pen for you
- pencils for the children

Skills Developed:

- triggering imaginative possibilities, creating new combinations and avoiding clichés
- playing with words and ideas

How to Play the Game

We have always had a strong faith in the ridiculous and playful as a crucial part of children's development. Play is unscripted and therefore an area for the individual to dabble within a safe context, the child trying out their linguistic legs to see what works and what does not. In a sense, all writing is a form of play.

In this game, the children become 'Authors of the Ridiculous'. The basic idea is to create a list of book titles that have never been written and probably never will because they are about impossible subjects.

Model how to play the game by writing the phrase: *The Author of the Ridiculous wrote…* with a few title suggestions so that children can see how the game works, e.g. *The Author of the Ridiculous wrote… the Dictionary of Miserable Clowns*.

Then split the class into pairs and give each pair the photocopiable page **Books Written by the Authors of the Ridiculous** for them to complete. Give the children a few minutes to jot down their ideas and then come together as a class again and encourage volunteers to share their ideas.

Examples

The Author of the Ridiculous wrote...

- *The Encyclopaedia of Silent Choirs.*
- *The Thesaurus of Cold Flames.*
- *The Boys' Book of Invisible Rainbows.*
- *The Girls' Book of Soft Concrete.*
- *The Anthology of Straight Corners.*
- *The Glossary of Disastrous Fortunes.*
- *The Compendium of Edible Rocks.*
- *The Notebook of Useful Nuisances.*

> **TIP**: Of course, children can make up any old silly ideas, such as *The Boys' Guide to Hamster Farming*, but encourage them to come up with impossible opposites such as *cold flames* or *truthful lies*. These are technically known as 'oxymorons' – which is a funny enough sounding word in itself.

Books Written by the Authors of the Ridiculous

The Album of_____

The Annual of_____

The Anthology of_____

The Atlas of_____

The Bestiary of_____

The Book of_____

The Booklet of_____

The Boys' Book of_____

The Comic of_____

The Compendium of_____

The Diary of_____

The Dictionary of_____

The Directory of_____

The Encyclopaedia of_____

The Essay of_____

The Girls' book of_____

The Glossary of_____

The Guide to_____

The Guidebook of_____

The Hardback of_____

The Journal of_____

The Ledger of_____

The List of_____

The Magazine of_____

The Newspaper of_____

The Notebook of_____

The Omnibus of_____

The Pamphlet of_____

The Paperback of_____

The Picture-book of_____

The Quarterly of_____

The Scroll of_____

The Sketchbook of_____

The Textbook of_____

The Thesaurus of_____

The Volume of_____

The Weekly of_____

The Wordbook of_____

9. Why Does the Sun Beam?

For the whole class.

Equipment:

- a whiteboard and a whiteboard pen for you

Skills Developed:

- the ability to use puns and word play

How to Play the Game

This is ideal as a quick starter to get everyone's minds whirring. Of course, there is a play on the word *sun beam* – meaning either *a sunbeam* or *the sun beaming*. Use the title of the game as a prompt for discussion about the different ways it could be interpreted before moving into brainstorming the answer with the class.

Example
Why does the sun beam?

Usually, you get the obvious and somewhat clichéd ideas about spreading light or happiness. However, encourage more interesting ideas based on the two different interpretations of the question:

Why does the sun beam? Meaning 1: Why does the sun generate light? *The sun beams to light up...* • *the dark corners of a forgotten box* • *the end of a cave* • *the tunnels beneath the city* • *the shadows that a block of flats casts* • *the Minotaur's labyrinth* • *the bags under a teacher's eyes*	*Why does the sun beam?* Meaning 2: Why does the sun smile? *The sun smiles because...* • *a cloud has just told it a joke* • *it is happy to see children playing* • *it has scared away the rain* • *it has just said goodbye to the moon* • *it has just made a rainbow*

As children come up with suggestions note these down on the whiteboard as this will help to generate further ideas.

Variation

- Ask the children further questions that involve word play.

    - *Why did the rain drop?*
    - *Why did the snow flake?*
    - *Why did the thunder rumble?*
    - *Why did the lightning strike?*

10. Invention from Imitation – Sentences

For the whole class working together and then independently.

Equipment:
- a whiteboard and a whiteboard pen for you
- writing journals and pencils for the children
- paper and coloured pens to display examples on the working wall

Skills Developed:
- rehearsing sentence patterns that might become a useful part of children's writing repertoire

How to Play the Game

This is such a simple idea, but it is like a revelation to many children, when you suggest to them that you look at different writers together, whose stories they love, to see how they have created different sentences.

It involves picking some intriguing sentence patterns from selected stories and imitating them, using the same underlying syntax. You can really sell the idea to the children by suggesting that they can begin to write 'in the style of' a writer who they admire, like Michael Morpurgo or Jacqueline Wilson!

Ask the children to suggest favourite sentences from books (they can also jot these down in their writing journals) and then invent new ones together through imitating the patterns found. Begin by doing this together as a class, writing down the original sentences and the new ones you have crafted together on the whiteboard. Children can then have a go themselves independently.

Examples
The following sentences show how we have moved from imitation to invention, in each case beginning with a very simple sentence:

Original sentence from a story:	Invention using the same pattern:
Thunder growled overhead.	*Snow whispered above.*
Rusted dustbins rattled in the wind, fences creaked and the rain drummed on car roofs.	*Wilted poppies shivered in the snow, trees leaned and the wind whipped across the road.*

Make this sort of invention a very regular feature so that the children learn that when writing they can innovate on sentence patterns that they already know, in order to write powerfully. Discuss the effect of the sentences – what works?

> **TIP:** You might wish to display some 'imitation to invention' sentences on the working wall for children to refer to during shared, guided and independent writing. In this way, children might experiment with different patterns, building up a repertoire.

Extension Activity
- This game can be extended to innovating on whole paragraphs in the same way. Some children find this helps them make an effective link from their reading into their writing.

11. Ping Pong 📷

For the whole class or the whole class organised into pairs or small groups.

Equipment:
- the image CD and an interactive whiteboard or an unusual object (for the Variation)

Skills Developed:
- inventing a simple story together

How to Play the Game

This activity is about collaboratively creating a story together. It is really useful for children who struggle with ideas of what to write about as they can feed off each other's ideas. You can play it as a whole class together, in pairs or in small groups.

Tell the children that they are going to make up a new story there and then. Everybody must add a word at a time, going round the circle one-by-one (or back and forth in the pair), until the story is complete.

It is a good idea to model the activity with a Teaching Assistant before children have a go. For example, you could start with *Once*, the Teaching Assistant would say *upon*, and so on. The more children play this game, the better they will become. It doesn't matter particularly if the story doesn't make sense, it's about exercising the creative imagination.

> 💡 **TIP**: When playing this with the class, you can increase the fun, by calling it the 'Hot Story', similar to the game 'Hot Potato,' if you've ever played that (passing an imaginary hot potato around the circle). Explain you have a very hot story in your hands that is eager to be told! You start the story and mime passing the 'hot' story on to the child sat next to you. They must then think as quickly as possible of the next word/part of the story and pass it on fast, to avoid a burn!

Variations
- Try developing the game by playing it sentence-by-sentence or chunk-by-chunk.

- You could use an image on the CD, or an unusual object as a starting point.

- Play the same game, BUT each word must start with the same letter. This will help with alliterative skills and encourage children to consider different choices of words from their usual 'go-to' ones.

Example
- *Belinda bought Brian beautiful bouncy balls because Ben bothered Brian by badly burning Brian's best ball.*

12. Unfortunately, Luckily

For the whole class organised into pairs.

Equipment:
- none needed

Skills Developed:
- creating sentences, using adverbs at the start
- developing dilemma and resolution playfully

How to Play the Game

This is a very old game, but one that is worth wheeling out every so often. It helps to fine tune children's ability to be inventive and has an edge of challenge too.

Organise the class into pairs and give each pair a basic proposition, such as, *Jack climbed the beanstalk.* Partner A then provides a dilemma beginning with the word *Unfortunately*, e.g. *Unfortunately, it was covered in grease.* Partner B counters this by inventing a solution, starting with the word *Luckily*, e.g. *Luckily, Jack was using ropes.* Partner A then comes back with another problem, *Unfortunately, the ropes were frayed and broke.* Again, Partner B counters this with a solution, e.g. *Luckily, Jack had developed the ability to fly and soared to the top with ease.* The contest continues in this vein until one or the other partner is defeated. Pairs may wish to come out and perform their contest for the rest of the class.

Variation
- Try playing this game with the children in groups sat in small circles. If anyone gets stuck they can say 'pass' and then the next child carries on with the challenge.

13. Impossible Suggestions 💿 📷

For the whole class organised into pairs.

Equipment:
- the audio CD and a CD player
- a story that the class knows well (if desired)
- a whiteboard and a whiteboard pen for you (if desired)
- paper and pencils for the children (if desired)
- the image CD and an interactive whiteboard (for the Variation)

Skills Developed:
- creating sentences and a story using unexpected ideas

How to Play the Game

Play this game once the children have become very experienced at telling a story. The idea is quite simple and involves introducing incongruous elements (or 'impossible suggestions') into a story. However, it is not as easy as one would imagine so it is worth trying the game out in the staffroom first of all! When you first start playing the story, it is best if children use a story they know as a starting point.

Introduce the game to the children by listening to it being played on the CD. Then organise the class into pairs. Partner A has to make up the start of a story (as a chunk), or retell the beginning of a story they know. Partner B intervenes after each chunk and says a word that has NOTHING to do with the text so far – an impossible suggestion. The challenge is for Partner A to incorporate the word in the next sentence (or chunk).

The game puts demands on both partners. Partner B has to step out of the logical flow of the story and rapidly think of something completely unexpected and Partner A then has to rapidly think of a way of using that within the story, whilst maintaining some sort of sense.

Example
Partner A: Once upon a time there was a mouse who lived in a shoe.
Partner B: Custard.
Partner A: The mouse's favourite food was custard.
Partner B: Moon.
Partner A: Now the mouse heard that the moon was made of custard so it decided to fly there…

The game continues like this until Partner A either finishes the story, or is unable to include the word suggestion from Partner B.

The ENORMOUS Book of Talk for Writing Games for KS2

Variations

- Try playing the game only using a specific word class for the impossible suggestions, e.g. *nouns, verbs, connectives or adjectives.*

- Vary the game by using cards with words on them that the children choose from a feely bag. They have to use the word they select. In this version, both Partner A and Partner B can work together to construct the chunk that includes the impossible suggestion.

- You can use images from the CD as a starting point for story ideas if children need it.

14. The Child of Impossible Suggestions

For the whole class organised into pairs.

Equipment:

- a story that the class knows well (if desired)
- a whiteboard and a whiteboard pen for you (if desired)

Skills Developed:

- creating sentences and a story using expected ideas

How to Play the Game

This game follows on from the previous one. You will probably find the previous game leads to much hilarity. The effect of this game is interesting because we have found that children tend to quieten down and concentrate even more. It is a good idea to model this game with a Teaching Assistant before children have a go themselves.

Once again, the children work in pairs. Partner A has to make up the start of a story (as a chunk), or retell the beginning of a story they know. Partner B intervenes after each chunk and says a word that might be *useful* to the teller and help to move the story forwards. Partner A then has to incorporate the word in the chunk.

The game puts demands on both partners. Unlike the previous game, Partner B has to enter the logical flow of the story and rapidly think of something that might help move the tale forwards. Partner A then has to rapidly think of a way of using that within the story. It is an interesting way of creating a joint tale.

Example
Partner A: Once upon a time there was a mouse who lived in a shoe.
Partner B: Cat.
Partner A: The mouse's main fear was the cat that lived nearby.
Partner B: Purring.
Partner A: One day the mouse woke to hear a low purring noise...

The game continues like this for as long as desired or until a complete story has been created.

TIPS: If the children find it hard, you can scaffold the role of Partner B by making a long list of words together. Of course, you will have to agree on a story type to do this.

It also helps if the children use a story mountain with connectives on it to structure their story and maintain flow. This is available in Pie's *Story Maker's Chest.*

15. Ping Pong Connectives

For the whole class or the whole class organised into pairs or small groups.

Equipment:
- the photocopiable page **(Connectives)**
- the audio CD and a CD player
- a whiteboard and a whiteboard pen for you
- mini whiteboards and pens for the children (for the Variation)
- a timer (for the Variation)

Skills Developed:
- making up a story using a range of connectives

How to Play the Game

This is similar to the *Ping Pong* game, but as the story moves around the group, or back and forth in the pair, each child has to construct a whole sentence beginning with a story connective from the photocopiable sheet **(Connectives)** on the next page.

Introduce the activity by listening to it being played on the CD before letting children have a go themselves in their pairs, groups or as a whole class. If the children have English as a new language or find using a range of connectives difficult, model using a new connective in a sentence with the children repeating the sentence and making up a few new similar ones. Let us suppose that you were introducing the word 'meanwhile'. You might say, "*Let's try this one, 'meanwhile'. It means 'at the same time'. I'll try and make a sentence up and then we can make up some similar ones.*

Meanwhile, the old man ran home.
Meanwhile, the tiger ate the dog's dinner.
Meanwhile, the teacher marked everyone's work.

Now you have a go at making some up in your pairs."

> **TIP:** If you have Pie's *KS1 Story Maker's Chest* then you could play the game with the bank of connective cards instead of giving each child a copy of the photocopiable page. Challenge the children to choose their connective randomly from the selection and find a way to incorporate it into their sentence.

Variations
- List key connectives on the whiteboard indicating a score for each, depending on its difficulty. The children play the game and note down the connectives they use and the score for each on their whiteboards, but the connective has to be used 'correctly' and it must make sense. Give them a time limit and see who gets the top score at the end.

- You can also play this game for non-fiction.

Connectives

STORY CONNECTIVES	NON-FICTION CONNECTIVES AND STARTERS	CONNECTIVES THAT COME IN THE MIDDLE OF SENTENCES
Once upon a time	Additionally	and
One day/morning/	Also	as a result
evening/night	Alternatively	but
Early one morning	Although	because
Late one evening	Before	for
First	Finally	how
Next	First	if
After	Furthermore	or
After a while	However	so
Before	In addition	so that
But	Many	that
At that moment	Most	to
Suddenly	All	until
Immediately	On the other hand	when
Without warning	So	where
In an instant	Some	which
Out of the blue	A few	while
Although	Then	who
However	The main	
Later	The majority	
So	The minority	
Soon	When	
As	Whenever	
As soon as	While	
Then	Whilst	
While		
Meanwhile		
When		
Whenever		
Eventually		
Finally		
In the end		

16. The Salty Umbrella 💿

For the whole class organised into pairs.

Equipment:
- the photocopiable page (**Preposition List**)
- the audio CD and a CD player
- paper and pencils or mini whiteboards and whiteboard pens for the children

Skills Developed:
- combining words to produce new images

How to Play the Game

Taking an interest in words and their power is crucial not just to building vocabulary, but also to becoming a writer. Each word has to be chosen with care in order to create an effect. Of course, one word on its own can be evocative, but the real excitement begins when you put two words together. Worlds of sound, meaning, memory, connotation and association clash together to create a new effect.

Many words become associated together and are often found in speech and writing. Take, for instance, the words *Once upon a time…* They flow comfortably into each other, giving the reader a moment to settle down in expectation. However, we can ambush the reader by creating new combinations: *Once upon a truth…* or even more unexpected, *Once upon a cabbage…*

It is often the moment when words come together that do not normally combine that the unexpected collision of meaning and rhythm forces the words out of their old habits into fresh possibilities. This game is called *The Salty Umbrella* because it is an odd word combination that forces the reader to stop and think.

Introduce the game by listening to it being played on the CD with the children. Then organise the children into pairs and give each child a copy of the photocopiable sheet (**Preposition List**) on page 66. Partner A then makes a list of three nouns and so too does Partner B (both children keeping their lists hidden from each other). They then put the words together in the exact order that they were written down. This is important because it is the random combination that is often most powerful. So if Partner A writes, *ballet, jealousy* and *harp* and Partner B writes *moon, Paris* and *rust*, when they are combined they end up with *ballet moon, jealousy Paris* and *harp rust*. The challenge they now have is to link each set of two words with a preposition from the photocopiable page (**Preposition List**).

Examples
- *The harp of rust.*
- *The harp with rust.*
- *The harp in the rust.*

Now let's stretch each idea out into some sort of story, to begin to make some sort of sense from it.

- *The harp of rust lay in the corner. Tania picked it up and wondered whether it would still work. She blew the cobwebs from it and plucked one string. Even though the metal strings had rusted, the sound was still pure.*

- *The harp with rusty strings lay unused for many years.*

- *In the corner lay a pile of ancient, rusty objects. However, one item caught her eye. It was a harp… and it was not rusty.*

You can make the game even more specific by challenging one partner to list one type of noun, and the other to list another type of noun. For example, you could ask Partner A to write a list of objects and Partner B to write a list of places. Let us imagine that Partner A writes *clock, mirror* and *key* and Partner B writes *palace, lake* and *star*. We end up with the following combinations: *clock palace, mirror lake*, and *key star*. Now the children can use the prepositions to link the pairs again, bearing in mind that the words can be combined either way round.

Examples
- *The clock of palaces.* OR *The palace of clocks.*
- *The mirror beside the lake.*
- *The key on the star.* OR *The star inside the key.*

Again, the pairs of children can take the ideas and turn them into a mini story or image.

- *Once there was a palace which had a thousand clocks in every room. Wherever you went, you could not escape the ticking of time. The ceilings and walls were all made of clocks. Even the floors were paved with clocks.*

- *Beside the lake lay a mirror. It was the same shape as the lake. Tania picked it up and stared into it. What she saw was quite unexpected.*

- *"But how can I open the tower and set Tania free?" asked the boy. The old man pointed up towards a distant star. "The key is on that star," he whispered, shaking his head, sadly.*

What is amazing about this idea is that with very little thought, some interesting stories will start to be created.

Variation

- Try a different version in which Partner A generates a list of characters and Partner B generates a list of containers. So, Partner A might write down *prince, thief* and *cat* and Partner B could have *jar, sack* and *prison*. This would lead to the following combinations: *prince jar, thief sack* and *cat prison*. Now the children can use the list of prepositions to combine these.

Examples

- *The prince in the jar.*
- *The sack of thieves.*
- *The cat outside the prison.*

They can then use these fragments to create a full story.

Preposition List

on	into	out of
with	next to	back of
of	by	to
in	from	among
inside	against	between
under	without	made of
beside	up	made from
below	upon	different to
on top of	over	near
beyond	until	far
behind	around	along
at	for	in front of
before	down	through
about	past	off
close to	across	

The ENORMOUS Book of Talk for Writing Games for KS2

17. The Story Restaurant 💿

For the whole class organised into pairs.

Equipment:
- the photocopiable page **(Story Menu)**
- the audio CD and a CD player
- paper and pencils for the children
- a die
- cards and pens to create menu cards (for the Variation)

Skills Developed:
- inventing a new story using basic ingredients

How to Play the Game

In this game, children use the 'ping pong' technique to invent a new story, chunk-by-chunk. It can be quite a challenging game so they will need plenty of practice and will definitely benefit from seeing the game modelled by you and a Teaching Assistant.

Introduce the game by letting the children listen to it being played on the CD. Then organise the class into pairs and give each pair the photocopiable sheet **(Story Menu)** on the next page, a die, paper and pencils. The children can then roll the die to select and write down their ingredients to include in their story: a character, a setting, an object, an animal and an event. So, if they rolled a three, they could choose a *Goblin* from the first 'Character' card, and so on until they have all five ingredients. Partner A should then begin by telling the first of chunk of the story, drawing on one or more of the elements they have selected. They should then pass the story to Partner B to continue. The game continues like this until all five of the elements have been included and the story is complete.

> 💡 **TIP**: This game makes a useful way to start a session or sequence of teaching in which the children are going to write their own story. You will notice that when children first have a go at this, they play around and just have fun. However, it is worth focusing them on creating a story that hangs together and flows in a logical sequence – which is harder. It can help if children begin by sketching a story map or board with a basic story. Then they use this to steadily make up their joint tale – section-by-section.

Variations
- You could give children a story genre that they have to stick to, e.g. *science-fiction, fantasy, traditional, thriller, ghost, action, adventure, domestic, school,* etc. Then they might consider the 'type' of story, e.g. *warning, beating the baddie, wishing, rags to riches, problem/resolution, journey, quest,* etc. Having made these decisions, children then choose ingredients that are appropriate, rather than making random selections using the die.

- You could create your own 'menu cards' with the children making suggestions of what to have on each.

Extension Activity
- When children are experienced at playing this game, they can choose several characters and settings to include in their story so that different characters interact with each other and the action moves from one place to another.

Story Menu

STORY MENU CARDS – CHARACTERS	STORY MENU CARDS – SETTINGS	STORY MENU CARDS – OBJECTS	STORY MENU CARDS – ANIMALS	STORY MENU CARDS – EVENTS
1. Ogre 2. Giant 3. Goblin 4. Dwarf 5. Elf 6. Fairy	1. Forest 2. Beach 3. Mountain 4. Cave 5. River 6. Stream	1. Needle 2. Spinning wheel 3. Thread 4. Rope 5. Ball 6. Knife	1. Ant 2. Cat 3. Dog 4. Snake 5. Hamster 6. Rabbit	1. A computer breaks down. 2. The road is blocked. 3. Someone breaks in. 4. A villain arrives. 5. A beanstalk appears. 6. A secret place is discovered.
1. Heroine 2. Hero 3. Villain 4. Bandit 5. Robber 6. Thief	1. Palace 2. House 3. Factory 4. Bus station 5. Playground 6. Park	1. Axe 2. Comb 3. Handkerchief 4. Tablecloth 5. Basket 6. Bag	1. Hare 2. Spider 3. Tiger 4. Lion 5. Fox 6. Wolf	1. A strange gift arrives. 2. Something precious is found. 3. Something precious is stolen. 4. A nosey relative visits. 5. Someone sets off to find something. 6. Someone has to carry something precious.
1. Soldier 2. Sailor 3. Teacher 4. Girl 5. Boy 6. Mum	1. Motorway 2. Classroom 3. Shopping centre 4. Market 5. Alley-way 6. Chip shop	1. Sack 2. Box 3. Lamp 4. Coin 5. Purse 6. Ring	1. Eagle 2. Robin 3. Stork 4. Pelican 5. Shark 6. Whale	1. A warning is broken. 2. Someone or something is transformed into an animal. 3. Someone is dared to be dangerous. 4. Bullies gang up. 5. A hiding place is discovered. 6. An alien needs protection.
1. Dad 2. Sister 3. Brother 4. Granddad 5. Grandma 6. Friend	1. Deserted house 2. Railway station 3. Distant star 4. Grandma's house 5. Kitchen 6. Shed	1. Cloak 2. Hat 3. Chair 4. Car 5. Cart 6. Apple	1. Salmon 2. Bird of paradise 3. Elephant 4. Giraffe 5. Donkey 6. Horse	1. A wish is granted. 2. Something valuable is lost. 3. An intruder appears. 4. A secret is discovered. 5. Someone is afraid of something that then happens. 6. Someone is pushed.
1. Traveller 2. Shop-keeper 3. Wizard 4. Farmer 5. Tailor 6. Baker	1. Tower 2. Swamp 3. Underground mine 4. Desert 5. Fairground 6. Cinema	1. Mirror 2. Key 3. Shoes 4. Boots 5. Bottle 6. Book	1. Cow 2. Mouse 3. Rat 4. Sheep 5. Badger 6. Flea	1. An unexpected visitor arrives. 2. A secret message arrives. 3. A baddie captures a good character. 4. Someone is lost and can't get home. 5. A magical item is discovered. 6. Someone is given superpowers for the day.

The ENORMOUS Book of Talk for Writing Games for KS2

18. The Story Channel

For the whole class or a small group.

Equipment:
- a digital camera or iPad for recording (if desired)

Skills Developed:
- vocalising a story
- quick thinking

How to Play the Game

This is a really fun, silly game that can be played as a whole class or in a small group. Tell children that they are presenters on the newest cool TV channel in story land: 'The Story Channel'. Their job is to make up a story to entertain the listeners, BUT they can only speak when you are pointing at them.

So, you point at one child who tells the start of their story and when you point at someone else, the first child stops talking and another starts. The aim is for each child to try and continue their story from the place they left it when they were last pointed at (despite several children telling parts of their stories in the meantime) and to try and string together a beginning, middle and end! In this way, the whole occasion is rather like someone switching channels and endlessly flicking between different stories, each one picking up where it left off!

If you have the equipment, filming the children will add to the excitement of it being a real TV Channel.

Variations
- Split the children into small groups. Say that the whole classroom is the television and that the different groups are the television channels. Give each group a type of channel (wildlife, history, news, etc.). Using the whole class, play the game as before – so if a child is on the history channel, they must tell a story relating to this subject when they are pointed at.

- Following on from the above Variation activity, organise each group so that they stand in a line. Point at the first person in the line who must start the story relating to their channel and then move along the line to the second person, then the third person, and so on. Each child will have to continue the bit of television commentary started by the person in front of them. Encourage the children to chat and practice beforehand as to what their television commentary is about.

19. Stanislavski's Questions 💿 📷

For the whole class or the whole class organised into small groups.

Equipment:
- the audio CD and a CD player
- the image CD and an interactive whiteboard (or a selection of pictures from magazines)
- a whiteboard and a whiteboard pen for you

Skills Developed:
- the ability to build and develop character

How to Play the Game

This game is based on the work of the famous theatre practitioner Stanislavski who was passionate about character and used questions to help create them.

Introduce the game by listening to it being played on the CD with the class. Then work with the children as a whole class or in groups, to answer these questions about a main character. This will help the children think more roundly about all elements of a character, not just their name!

Who am I? Think about age, sex, what the character looks like, what their background is, what their likes/dislikes are, whether they are sad, happy, worried, hopeful, etc. *(Dan the zookeeper)*	Where am I? Think about the immediate circumstances of the character's setting – smells, sounds, colours, tastes, things near to them, things in the distance. *(At the zoo, in the penguin enclosure)*
What do I want? What is motivating the character? What is their goal? *(To catch a penguin that has a poorly foot)*	How shall I go about it? How does the character behave to get what they want? *(Using a big net, Dan catches the penguin, but is very scared of it!)*
When am I? Think about what time of day, week, month, year it is. *(A sunny Monday morning, Spring 2013)*	

Try and make the children be specific and inventive when creating a main character. They might have a strange obsession, e.g. *stamp-collecting, knitting socks, catching butterflies; always wear a certain item of clothing (a bright bogey-green t-shirt); or maybe they always have a certain phrase they always say ("Oh bother!").*

If needed, use an image from the CD or a magazine to stimulate their visual imagination.

The ENORMOUS Book of Talk for Writing Games for KS2

20. Story from a Photo 📷

For the whole class.

Equipment:

- the image CD and an interactive whiteboard (or pictures from a magazine)
- writing journals and pencils for the children
- a range of interesting objects (for the Variation)

Skills Developed:

- inventing from a visual prompt

How to Play the Game

Choose a photo with a person in it, either from the image CD or a magazine. With the class, make up a back story about the person in the photograph, using these types of questions to prompt ideas.

- *Who is this person?*
- *Where do they live?*
- *How old are they?*
- *What do they do as a job?*
- *What makes this person special?*
- *Who is taking the photograph?*
- *What happened just before this photograph?*
- *What will happen just after this photograph?*

Then get the children to write a story in full of what is happening in the moment of the photo, or what happened just before or what may happen after.

Variations

- This game can be played in many different ways. For example, you could bring an interesting object in and ask the class a series of questions about it.

  - *Who found this object?*
  - *Where was it found?*
  - *How old is it?*
  - *How much is it worth?*
  - *Who did it belong to?*
  - *Does it have any special powers?*

- Repeat the same game with pictures showing settings or events.

21. Professor Bob's Museum 📷

For the whole class.

Equipment:

- the image CD and an interactive whiteboard or a range of unusual objects
- a whiteboard and a whiteboard pen for you
- access to computers and the internet
- a digital camera or iPad for filming 'Professor Bob'

Skills Developed:

- developing an imaginative context
- unfolding narrative from objects and collections

How to Play the Game

Show the class lots of photos of unusual objects from the image CD, or a range of concrete unusual items (curios found abroad are usually best). Tell the children that you have bought them from *Professor Bob's Emporium of Strange Finds* and that he gathered these during his travels around the world.

Discuss with the class where the esteemed Professor Bob may have found these objects and what their function might be. Are they magical objects? Did Professor Bob have a frightening experience finding any of the objects and bringing them back to England?

Develop the game by writing a class story about Professor Bob's travels across the globe to bring back the rarest objects to England. You could relate the objects to other subjects you are studying with the children and continue the game by writing letters to them in role as Professor Bob! You can make this as inventive as possible, showing the children 'letters' or 'emails' from the Professor along with photos from his travels. You could even start a blog for him. In each piece of correspondence you can weave in activities for the children to do, perhaps Bob requires some information about something, or maybe children could write back with made-up stories of their travels and experiences.

One school (thanks to Honiton Primary) uses this sort of idea as an unfolding narrative that develops across the whole year. The Professor sends curiosities back from his travel, but often needs help with information sent to him. At various points, he may also need collections of stories to keep him entertained or perhaps to charm a disgruntled emperor.

> 💡 **TIP:** Try using film clips of Bob talking to camera – this can be handy if a member of staff has an especially grizzled family member who might play the role. Add in extra flavour by using school trips where a message in a bottle might be found from Bob who has become stranded on an island!

22. In a Dark, Dark House 💿 📷

For the whole class organised into pairs.

Equipment:

- the audio CD and a CD player
- the image CD and an interactive whiteboard
- a range of objects (for the Variation)
- writing journals and pencils for the children (for the Extension Activity)

Skills Developed:

- creating and developing a setting
- starting the action in a story

How to Play the Game

This game is designed to help develop a setting and begin to get the action going in a story. It is based on the old traditional 'jump' story, *In a dark, dark house, there is a dark, dark room, and in the dark room there is...* These tales are known as 'jump' stories because they usually end with the teller shouting something out and making the listeners 'jump' with surprise.

Introduce the game to the children by listening to it being played on the CD. Then organise the class into pairs and ask them to think of a setting where they would like their story to take place. Alternatively, you can use a setting from the image CD and display it on the interactive whiteboard. In their pairs the children should begin by describing the setting, bouncing ideas back and forth of what they might be able to see, each adding a new addition to the setting.

<u>Example</u>
Partner A: In a dark warehouse, there is a table.
Partner B: In a dark warehouse there is a table and beside the table is a box.
Partner A: In a dark warehouse there is a table and beside the table there is a box and in the corner of the room there is one small, grimy window.
Partner B: In a dark warehouse there is a table and beside the table there is a box, in the corner of the room there is one small, grimy window and inside the box there is a feather.

And so on...

Once the setting has been sufficiently described, change tack and ask the pairs to make something happen in their setting. To do this, Partner A should use the phrase, *At that moment...* Then as more action is introduced, each child should use the phrase, *After that...* for each new event.

Example

Partner A: In a dark warehouse there is a table and beside the table there is a box, in the corner of the room there is one small, grimy window and inside the box there is a feather. At that moment, the door opens...

Partner B: After that, a very thin man enters.

Partner A: After that, the thin man strides across the room towards the box.

Partner B: After that, he kneels down in front of the box and strokes the surface lovingly.

Partner A: After that, he carefully opens the box and very delicately he pulls out the feather.

Partner B: After that, he holds the feather up as if it was a dandelion and he blows upon it and all the tiny, tiny bits of the feather begin to drift off.

And so on...

Variation

- Provide objects that have to be included in the setting.

Extension Activity

- Develop this activity so that an entire story is told from start to finish. Once the children have come up with ideas for their story, encourage them to map it out and then retell it to the rest of the class, perhaps using the 'ping pong' technique.

23. Guided Journey – Forest

For the whole class and then the whole class organised into pairs.

Equipment:

- a large space where children can sit comfortably
- writing journals and pencils for the children (for the Extension Activity)
- writing journals and pencils for the children (for the Extension Activity)

Skills Developed:

- imagining scenes

How to Play the Game

This activity involves the children sitting and staring into space while you build an imaginative journey for them to see inside their heads. Make sure everyone is settled and still – no fidgeting allowed. Then get the children to stare at something dull like the carpet or ceiling, or close their eyes.

Begin the guided journey by talking slowly, in a low but audible voice, keeping an even tone. Describe the journey and, as you do, invite the children to try to see it in their own minds. Remember to use words that will be within their vocabulary and experience, otherwise the imagining cannot take place.

Example

You are standing at the edge of a forest. The trees are very tall. They tower high above you... Look up and you can see the tops. A few black birds are circling round. Now look in between the trees into the forest. It is dark in there. Walk forwards into the forest. The shadows close in around you. You can feel it getting colder as you leave the sunlight behind. You tread carefully on the forest floor – it is mossy. Green moss. Now between the tall trees ahead you can see a clearing. There is a small cottage made of wood. Smoke is coming out of the stone chimney. You step into the clearing where it is sunny. Go up to the door... Knock on the door... Who opens it? What do they say? They have something to give you... What is it?

Once you have created the scene and introduced some action, it works well to pause at this point. Now it is up to the children to continue the fantasy and talk through what happens next with the person sitting beside them. In the above example, they would talk about who opened the door, what they say and what they gave the children. Let them chat for a short while and then hear some of their ideas.

Extension Activity

- Ask the children to try and write down the journey they went on in their minds, as an opening for a story.

24. Guided Journey – Building

For the whole class and then the whole class organised into pairs.

Equipment:

- a large space where children can sit comfortably
- writing journals and pencils for the children (for the Extension Activity)

Skills Developed:

- imagining scenes

How to Play the Game

Follow the instructions for *Guided Journey – Forest*, but this time focus on a special building. Try palaces, gloomy dungeons, ancient buildings, factories, tower blocks, etc. You could even use places that are of local interest, or places mentioned in a story you are studying.

Example

You are standing outside a ruined palace. The stone walls tower high above you, but are crumbling. You walk along the wall until you find a place where you can scramble over the stones. Inside it is quite silent. You are standing in a large room. High above there are wooden beams. You can see several owls sitting on a beam looking down at you. The walls are hung with faded tapestries and paintings. There is a long table in front of you. On the table is a letter. You walk over to the table leaving a trail of dusty footprints. Cobwebs hang across the backs of the chairs. You pick up the letter and open it. There is a sentence written there… You can see what it says… You turn around, but blocking your way is a person standing there… looking at you… So you say to them…

As before, once you have created the scene and introduced some action, pause the description. Now it is up to the children to continue the fantasy and talk through what happens next with the person sitting beside them. In the above example, they would talk about what was written in the letter, who blocked the way, what they looked like and what they said to them. Let them chat for a short while and then hear some of their ideas.

Variation

- Vary the game by trying different settings, both exterior and interior, e.g. *on the beach, through a jungle, in a city, through a tunnel, through countryside fields,* etc.

Extension Activity:

- At certain points, ask the children to imagine parts of the setting and write down what they see. Prompt their imaginations and try and make them be as specific and detailed as possible. They then begin to become responsible for part of the invention themselves. At the end, get them to share their observations with each other.

Example

You might say:

Then Billy approaches the door… What kind of door do you see, everyone? Is it small or tall? What is it made out of? Wood? Metal? What colour is it?

Next Billy opens the door and behind it he sees a garden. What is in the garden? Are there flowers or trees or is the ground bare and parched?

Once the journey is complete, ask the children to try and repeat the journey back to their partner, out loud. Then encourage them to write it out in their writing journals to use as part of a story.

25. Guided Journey – Dilemmas

For the whole class.

Equipment:
- a large space where children can sit comfortably
- a guided journey (that you have prepared beforehand)
- a skeleton story relating to the guided journey (that you have prepared beforehand)
- a whiteboard and pen for you
- a story that the class knows well (for the Variation)

Skills Developed:
- learning how to insert dilemmas into stories and how to solve them

How to Play the Game

Follow the instructions for the two previous *Guided Journey* games, but this time as the journey evolves, insert dilemmas into the story and then discuss with the children how each one can be solved. Try and get them to come up with a few options, choose one, then continue the story. Children are then directly helping with the creation of the story.

> **TIP**: Try and have the skeleton of a story prepared so that you have a vague beginning, middle and end to stick to!

Example
Dilemma:
At that moment, the door slammed and John was trapped inside the shed!

Solutions:
John shouts and someone comes to let him out.
John manages to break the lock.
John climbs out of a window.
John finds a secret passage out the shed, into another world...

Variation
- Try 'magpying' (taking) the start of a story from a well-known tale, picture book, film or novel. Start it off, then pause at a moment of dilemma and decide with the class on a different tack or solution to the one in the original version.

26. Soundscapes 📷

For the whole class.

Equipment:
- the image CD and an interactive whiteboard
- a large space where children can sit comfortably
- a whiteboard and pen for you
- writing journals and pencils for the children
- objects from the classroom or instruments (for the Variation)
- a poem or a passage from a book (for the Extension Activity)

Skills Developed:
- describing a setting through sound effects

How to Play the Game

Make sure all the children are sat comfortably (in a circle on the floor is best). Choose a setting from the image CD and give the children a couple of minutes to look at it. Then ask them to close their eyes and think of a sound effect they associate with that setting. Prompt them with ideas for sounds if they need it. Next, invite them to make the sound they have chosen (they can change or develop their sounds if they like) altogether as a class. So, they could make a gentle whistling sound to mimic the wind, or they could make the creak of a door opening. Very soon you will hear the setting come alive in the classroom!

After you've played this game, ask the children to describe the sound effects that they heard in as much detail as possible. Jot these down on the whiteboard and children can also write these in their journals for future reference to use when describing sounds in stories. The more you play this game, the bigger your 'bank of sound effects' will be for the children to log.

Example
Setting – A Haunted House

- *The wild, whistling wind through windows*
- *Creaking, squeaking floorboards*
- *Doors slamming shut*
- *A clock tick-tocking*
- *A loud, ferocious cackle!*
- *A cat scratching at the door*

Variations
- Settings that would work well for this activity include a fairground, a beach, a toy shop, a jungle, Grandma's kitchen, etc.

- Use objects in the classroom, or instruments to create the sounds.

- Add actions to the sound effects for fun and emphasis.

Extension Activities
- Perform a poem or short passage adding sound effects – either to support the meaning or as a background rhythm.

- Ask a volunteer to mime a little scene with sound effects added in, e.g. *someone might mime turning on a tap, filling a kettle, frying an egg, brushing their teeth, using a computer, turning on a radio, listening to the kettle boiling, pouring water into a cup*, etc.

- Make up a story as a class in which you incorporate sounds, e.g. *the wind in the trees as the main character walks through the forest; the distant sound of wood being chopped; a low growl of a wolf; the sound of a horse*, etc.

- Invent sounds for punctuation as a class. Perform a poem or read a passage from any book, performing the punctuation as sounds. This can be very funny.

27. Memory Pebbles

For the whole class working in pairs, then in small groups and then independently.

Equipment:
- pebbles from the beach of a reasonable size
- permanent markers
- paper and pencils for the children
- bags, boxes or postcards (for the Variation)

Skills Developed:
- selecting key words to capture a memory
- honing memory skills

How to Play the Game

The idea with this game is for the children to select a memory, generate key words that capture the memory and write them onto the pebble in a decorative fashion. We've tried memory pebbles about the following and all have worked well:

- a favourite place
- a special person
- an important event in my life

Begin by asking the children to 'picture' in their minds the memory that they are going to use as a basis for their pebble writing. Have a moment or two of silence as they recall the person, place or event. Put children in pairs to describe their memories to each other. Then put them into small circles with each child taking it in turns to retell their memory. The simple action of telling and retelling their memories will help them to think of the key words associated with it. They should then work alone and list these words on paper. Encourage them to be adventurous in their descriptive words, so the word 'sparks' could suggest an explosively good time!

The difficulty comes as there is only limited space on the pebble. On their list of words they could circle the ones that capture the essence of the experience. These can then be written decoratively onto the pebble.

Variation
- Memories can also be kept in memory bags, boxes or written onto postcards.

28. Special Objects

For the whole class organised into pairs.

Equipment:

- objects, letters or music brought in by the children from home
- writing journals and pencils for the children

Skills Developed:

- using the memory to generate story ideas
- using objects as inspiration for stories

How to Play the Game

Children's own experiences are a great way into story making. They find writing about something they know so much easier, and of course the writing is often higher quality with rich descriptions, fuller characters and more realistic dialogue – as well as better structured plots.

Ask the children to bring in something from home that triggers a memory or tells a story about an experience they have had. It could be a toy, a photograph, a piece of music that takes them back to a specific event, a postcard or letter, a favourite garment, etc. Encourage them to share their memory with a partner focusing on what happened, when it happened, where it happened, who was there, how they learnt from the experience and how it has changed them. Confident children might also like to share their stories with the rest of the class. Children can then turn their experiences into a short story.

Variation

- Children could swap their objects with a partner (respecting other people's property) and then create a story using that object – so a new character and tale is invented from being inspired by the object.

29. Picturing a Memory

For the whole class working independently and then the whole class organised into pairs.

Equipment:

- writing journals and pencils for the children
- paper and art and craft materials

Skills Developed:

- harnessing a memory to be used as inspiration for writing
- descriptive and listening skills

How to Play the Game

Everyone talks about creativity and the role of the imagination in education, but little time is spent considering how to encourage its development. Can it be strengthened?

The memory is an amazing and undervalued aspect of becoming a writer. In some way, we are our memories. If you take away someone's memory then there is not much left. Anyone who has had a relative suffering from a form of dementia will know that it is the memory that makes us rich and interesting human beings. Without memory, we are hollow vessels.

This game is useful to play early in the year because it helps to generate memories that can later on be used when writing. Writers often use places, people and events that they have experienced in their own writing. Why bother trying to invent something new when there is a perfectly decent memory that can be drawn upon? Furthermore, a memory may be so potent that the writer can use it to make the writing sound real. This often comes from recalling specific details.

In this game, you ask the children to think of a memory. Get everyone settled comfortably and then you can begin. The children have to be silent. They should find something to look at – not something bright and busy as that will draw their attention outward and you want them to see into their minds. They need to look at a blank wall, a carpet, a spot on their table. They should then try and revisit the memory in the minds, reliving the experience, hearing the sounds, feeling the breeze and recalling the feelings. If a thought creeps in and destroys the image, they need to come back to it.

This intense recalling helps to build their imaginative capacity in terms of holding something in their minds for close inspection. Most people can only manage a few seconds at first, but this can be improved with practice.

Once children have visited the experience in their minds, you can organise the class into pairs and get the children to tell each other what they saw, so that the memory is turned into words. Children can then write their memories out in full as a story, or create a piece of art that captures that memory.

Variation
- Ask children to describe each other's memories – this will test their listening and retelling skills!

Extension Activity
- Use the memories to make a Memory Map. Everyone knows about Mind Maps thanks to the pioneering work of Edward de Bono. These are an interesting strategy for drawing ideas, extending, linking and developing them. We like the way you can see your thinking pinned upon the page. To create their Memory Maps, children simply draw themselves in the centre of a large piece of paper and then have branches leading out which might relate to different times in their lives – before school, nursery, Key Stage 1, etc. They could also add on other branches – holidays, relatives, moving house, etc. Gradually they add on memories – these can be drawn or just added with a word or two. The children should show each other their maps and explain memories – this helps to generate new ideas and children will keep recalling more to add to their map. Encourage them to make the maps as decorative and colourful as they like.

30. Time-line Tales
For the whole class working independently and then the whole class organised into pairs.

Equipment:
- long strips of paper and pencils for the time-lines
- a whiteboard and a whiteboard pen for you (for the Extension Activity)
- writing journals and pencils for children (for the Extension Activity)

Skills Developed:
- harnessing memories as potential for story invention

How to Play the Game
This activity involves the children using strips of paper to create time-lines of their lives. It may help to share a list of different categories the children could include in their time-lines and discuss some of your own memories.

A list of reminders might include the following areas:

A time I was in trouble.	A family celebration.
Moving home.	My grandparents.
Moving school.	Something that scared me.
Losing something that was important to me.	An April Fool's day trick.
Telling a lie.	Something I find easy/difficult.
A funny thing that happened.	My best holiday or day trip.

Children could take the time-lines home and fill in details with the help of their parents and carers. Of course, the past is a sensitive issue for some children so this needs to be handled with care. On the other hand, some children may need to record difficult issues. Pie remembers one boy writing, *I was a brother, but the other one died*. He signalled that this was private by writing a capital 'P' beside the memory.

Once children have created their time-lines, they can work in pairs and tell each other a few memories. Confident children might also like to share some experiences with the rest of the class.

Extension Activity
- Get the children to find a memory on their time-line and move from silent visualising the event straight into 'burst' writing. It is a good idea to model this process first by choosing one of your memories and 'burst' writing about it. 'Burst' writing involves writing at full tilt as fast as possible to capture the snapshot. Children shouldn't worry about tidiness or spelling, just hold the memory and inspect it, then dash the words down on the page to capture it.

31. This Evening

For the whole class organised into pairs.

Equipment:
- none needed

Skills Developed:
- thinking more inventively about word choice

How to Play the Game

This game requires the children to really think about their word choice to describe events and encourages them to use richer, more inventive language. Organise the class into pairs and ask each pair to discuss with each other what they will be doing that evening (*how they'll get home, what they might eat, what they will do, etc.*), but the conversation MUST NOT feature any words beginning with the letter 'S'. It's harder than you think and a good way to get children to use words to describe things that they might not normally choose. Ask a few pairs to demonstrate their conversations and see if you can catch them out!

Variation
- Try it with another letter, 'T' is a good choice.

32. Yes/No Game

For the whole class organised into pairs.

Equipment:
- none needed

Skills Developed:
- thinking more inventively about word choice

How to Play the Game

Children love this game! As with *This Evening*, it is an excellent way of stretching children to be more inventive with their language. Put the class into pairs and then ask one partner in each pair to be the 'Asker' and one to be the 'Answerer'. The 'Asker' can then ask any question they like to their partner on a topic you have given them to talk about, e.g. *holidays, weekends, hobbies,* etc. The rule of the game is that the 'Answerer' can say anything except 'yes' or 'no.' See how long it takes for the 'Answerer' to be caught out!

Example
Asker: Did you enjoy your holiday?

Answerer: I did.

Asker: Did you really?

Answerer: I just said so.

Asker: Was it sunny?

Answerer: It was not.

Asker: Did you mind?

Answerer: That was fine by me.

And so on...

Variation
- Make the game harder by choosing some more words that are not allowed to be spoken while playing.

33. Character Cards

For the whole class.

Equipment:
- a pack of playing cards
- writing journals and pencils for the children

Skills Developed:
- developing simple character traits and personalities

How to Play the Game

This game is good to help children develop characters and their relationships with other characters. Give each child a card and then explain that the number on their card determines how confident or scared their character is (so a high number like a 9 would mean a very confident, brave character, whereas a number 3 would be quaking in their boots). The colour red or black could determine whether the character is a good character, or a bad character. Get the children to write a short character profile, inspired by the status their cards has determined.

Variation
- The colours and numbers can mean anything. So the colour could determine if the character is a boy or a girl and the number could determine how happy or sad they are, or rich or poor. It's up to you!

Extension Activities
- You could get everyone to write a short story about a day in the life of their character.

- Give each child another card and ask the children to talk about what may happen if the two characters met.

34. Fault/Help/Hinder

For the whole class.

Equipment:
- a whiteboard and a whiteboard pen for you
- a story that the class knows well (for the Variation)

Skills Developed:
- developing characters that are more complex and have personality traits or 'faults' which may become key to a story

How to Play the Game

Invent a character with the children – just creating a name and age is all that is needed at this stage, e.g. *James who is nine years old.* Then discuss with the children a 'fault' that the character may have and how it might BOTH help and hinder them in a story.

Example
Fault: James is a very greedy boy.

Help: A villain captures a Princess and says he'll only release her if someone can eat all the pies in the pie shop! James eats all the pies!

Hinder: James has to deliver an important present for his mother but opens the present, sees it is jam tarts and eats them all! What he didn't know was that his mother was sending the tarts to her enemy and poisoned them with magic dust, turning him into a jam tart!

Variation
- Take a story you are working on and look at a character from that. How may giving this character a fault add to the story?

35. Facts and Lies

For the whole class organised into pairs.

Equipment:
- none needed

Skills Developed:
- developing the imagination

How to Play the Game

This is a great game for helping children move from talking and writing about real life, to something that is invented. Put the children into pairs. Choose a topic for them, e.g. *what I did on holiday*. Ask the pairs to discuss this topic with each other. Then, ask them to come up with a convincing lie to add into the mix, e.g. *I swam with dolphins.*

The next stage of the game is to ask the pairs to tell the whole class about what each other did on holiday, mixing in some facts and some lies, e.g. *Freya went to Florida and stayed in a hotel, then she went to Disneyland and she made friends with a dolphin*. If the class think something is a lie, they shout out *LIE!*

36. That Didn't Happen

The whole class organised into pairs.

Equipment:
- none needed

Skills Developed:
- quick thinking
- recognising that there are lots of options for where to take a story and that the first idea is not always the best
- using reality as a starting point for invention

How to Play the Game

Put the children into pairs. The children should then take it in turns to tell each other what they did at the weekend. Their partner can interrupt them at certain points and say *that didn't happen*, at which point the teller has to change what happened and introduce some fantasy into the reality.

Example
Partner A: At the weekend I went swimming with my Mum and I went down a big water slide.

Partner B: That didn't happen.

Partner A: Okay, I wanted to go on the water slide, but slipped over before I reached it! Then my Mum came to see if I was alright.

Partner B: That didn't happen.

Partner A: Okay, a lifeguard rushed over to see what had happened.

And so on...

37. You Have It/No, You Have It!

For the whole class organised into pairs or the whole class organised into two groups.

Equipment:

- a range of interesting objects, e.g. *a box, a jewel, a letter, some fake money, a feather,* etc.
- writing journals and pencils for the children (for the Extension Activity)

Skills Developed:

- persuasion, constructing a clear, inventive argument

How to Play the Game

You can do this as a whole class (split into two groups) or in pairs. Ask one child from the pair (or one group) to select an object from the range you have provided and put forward reasons why the other person/half of the class, MUST take the object. Encourage the children to be really inventive as to why they want to be rid of the object, and what they can say to persuade the others to take it.

Example

Partner/Team A: I really think you should take this, it would look lovely in your house.

Partner/Team B: No, you must have it, I've simply no room for it.

Partner/Team A: But you could use it to feed your pet reindeer.

Partner/Team B: I think that actually your babysitter would love it for her birthday.

And so on...

When one partner or team runs out of reasons to make the other take it, or the other partner or team runs out of reasons as to why they shouldn't take it, swap roles and continue for as long as desired.

> **TIP:** Try and get the child or team to become more and more inventive, e.g. *If you melt this down, I've heard it becomes the most tasty dragon food for your pet dragon.*

Variation

- Play the same game, but this time the child or team has to persuade the other why they MUST keep the object for themselves, e.g. *It'll help cure my sick friend; I've been wanting this my whole life; I'll pay you a rich sum of money,* etc.

Extension Activity

- The children could then write a story about a character who has an object they desperately want to get rid of. Or about a character who desperately wants something – how do they go about getting it, what tactic do they use?

The ENORMOUS Book of Talk for Writing Games for KS2

38. Butcher and Customer

For the whole class organised into pairs.

Equipment:
- none needed

Skills Developed:
- helps children to become succinct in their word choices

How to Play the Game

This is an excellent activity for helping children to choose the right words and avoid using unnecessary extras, which can often be a problem in writing. Organise the class into pairs and ask each pair to act out a scene: one playing the 'Butcher', and the other playing the 'Customer'. Give them the following scenario to act out: *the customer is returning some meat to the butcher.* HOWEVER, the children can only use FOUR words per line, but the scene must still make sense.

Example
Partner A: I'm returning this meat.

Partner B: Not very good, Sir?

Partner A: No it really wasn't.

Partner B: I'm very sorry, Sir.

Partner A: Well, I'm very angry.

Partner B: How can I help?

Continue like this until a satisfactory solution has been found for the customer, or until one player uses more than four words and therefore loses the game.

 TIP: This can be performed sat down and no great acting is required.

Variation
- Change the characters and scenario. It could be set in a clothes shop, a restaurant, a dentist surgery, etc.

39. Who Will Buy?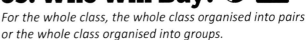

For the whole class, the whole class organised into pairs or the whole class organised into groups.

Equipment:
- the audio CD and a CD player
- the image CD and an interactive whiteboard (or a box full of interesting objects)

Skills Developed:
- persuading an audience
- developing the imagination
- using objects in stories

How to Play the Game

This simple game is a great way of introducing objects into a story. You can play this with children as individuals, pairs or in groups, depending on how brave they are!

Introduce the game to the children by listening to it being played on the CD together. Then ask a child (from the whole class, pair or group) to pick an object from the selection – or use an object on the image CD instead. They should then act in role as a travelling salesperson and think of inventive ways of selling the object to people they meet on their journey, i.e. the rest of the class, their partner or the rest of the group.

Example
Object: *A ball.*

Possible ways to sell it:

- *You must buy this ball because it contains magic dust and if you're in danger you simply pop the ball and release the dust to help you!*

- *This ball was found in a dark cave and is the eyeball of a rare creature!*

- *You must buy this ball because if you throw the ball in the air it acts as a spy camera and when you catch it, it plays you back what is surrounding you.*

Variation
- If you are working on a story you could use objects that would be relevant to the characters, e.g. *selling a toothbrush to the Big Bad Wolf because he needs to be attractive to future dinner prospects!*

40. Why I Should Have A Million Pounds

For the whole class, the whole class organised into pairs or the whole class organised into groups.

Equipment:
- paper and pencils or mini whiteboards and whiteboard pens for the children

Skills Developed:
- expanding the imagination
- the ability to talk and write persuasively

How to Play the Game
This game can be played with individuals, pairs or groups. Explain to the class you have one million pounds to give away, but will only give it to the person, pair or group who convinces you that they really should have the money! Ask them to think of some ideas together, jot these down and then present their case to you. They can be as imaginative as possible.

Example
- *I need money for my rare multi-coloured zebra to have his coat repainted!*

Variation
- You could look at one of the characters in a story you are working on and argue on behalf of them why they should have the money!

41. I'm In Prison, Get Me Out Of Here!

For the whole class organised into pairs.

Equipment:
- none needed

Skills Developed:
- retelling a story from a child's own perspective

How to Play the Game
This game helps children to tell a story from a particular character's perspective as well as honing their persuasive skills to get the outcome they desire.

Organise the class into pairs. Explain that one of the pair has been arrested by the police by mistake. The other is their friend who has come to find out what happened and try and get them released! The 'arrested' person should make up a story for their partner explaining why they have been mistakenly arrested, *(and then I was chased by a dog and so to escape I ran into the palace garden…)*. Their partner then tries to remember and tell the whole story back to the rest of the class in their own words *(Steve is in prison because one day he…)*. Based on their explanation of events, the class can act as jury and decide whether to release the prisoner or not.

> **TIP:** Sensitivity is required when playing this game as there may be children with relatives or family friends in prison. You could always change the scenario to being mistakenly caught by the head-teacher, parent, neighbour, etc.

Variations
- Instead of retelling the story in their own words, challenge the children to an imitation exercise – they have to retell the story EXACTLY how it was told to them, using the same words and gestures!

- You can vary this with any situation. The key is to get the children retelling a story they have heard in their own words.

42. Birthday Party 1 – Introducing Dilemmas

For the whole class.

Equipment:

- a flip-chart and pen for you

Skills Developed:

- developing the ability to insert dilemmas into stories
- problem solving

How to Play the Game

This game introduces children to the idea of 'rituals' and 'traditions' of everyday life and how disrupting rituals in their writing, can make their stories more exciting.

Hold a class discussion with the children about all the elements that make up a birthday party (guests arriving, playing party games, blowing out candles on a cake, etc.). Note these down on the flip-chart in chronological order (from the arrival at the party, to leaving at the end) – this will help them with their ability to create a sequential narrative.

Examples

- *Friends arriving at party*
- *Friends giving presents*
- *Opening presents*
- *Having a drink of squash and lemonade*
- *Playing party games*
- *Eating party food*
- *The cake – singing and blowing out candles*

Next, choose one of the elements of the birthday party and brainstorm a variety of ways that element could be 'disrupted', or a dilemma could be introduced.

Example

- *Opening presents.*

Disruptions

- *No one has bought you any presents!*
- *Everybody has bought you the same present!*
- *You open one of the presents, and there's a spider inside!*
- *Someone has stolen all of your presents!*
- *Your grandmother has bought you an expensive breakable present and you break it!*
- *You cut yourself on the wrapping paper and get blood all over your presents!*
- *You spill squash on an electronic present and break it!*
- *Your friend buys you a jumper, but it's ten sizes too big!*

You can continue like this, looking at other parts of the ritual and introducing dilemmas for each one.

> **TIP:** Not all children will have the same sort of birthday parties for financial or religious reasons. However, all will probably have had some sort of celebration. Make sure all experiences are valued and considered. Try and make the children be as specific as possible in their examples.

Variation

- You can apply this game to any 'ritual' e.g. *the breakfast routine, a day at school, Christmas, going to the cinema,* etc.

43. Birthday Party 2 – Solving Dilemmas

For the whole class.

Equipment:

- a flip-chart and pen for you
- writing journals and pencils for the children

Skills Developed:

- developing the ability to resolve problems in stories

How to Play the Game

As going through the ritual of a birthday party may have taken some time, this game can be played separately, but is related to the first so don't throw the flip-chart paper away! Look at the dilemmas that were introduced in *Birthday Party 1* and brainstorm with the class the different options for how each problem could be solved.

> **TIP:** It's important to come up with more than one solution to show children their first idea may not always be the best or most interesting.

Once each dilemma has a few solutions, why don't you get the children to write the story of a birthday party, using some of the problems and dilemmas you came up with as a class? Of course it's even better if they create their own. They can be as imaginative as they like, so goblins eating the cake are allowed at this birthday!

Example

- *Opening presents*

Dilemma

- *No one has bought you any presents!*

Solutions

- *Your Mum tells you to go and look under your bed and she'd hidden some extra presents there.*
- *Your fairy godmother turns all the candles on the cake into presents.*
- *Your friends tell you they haven't bought you presents because they're taking you to the best toy shop in the world so you can choose them yourself!*

Variation

- If you have looked at other 'rituals' going wrong (*the breakfast routine, a day at school, going to the cinema,* etc.) find solutions for these too.

44. Story Openings

For the whole class.

Equipment:

- the photocopiable page **(Story Openings)**
- a whiteboard and a whiteboard pen for you
- writing journals and pencils for the children

Skills Developed:

- generating openings for stories

How to Play the Game

Give each child the photocopiable sheet **(Story Openings)** on the next page. Read aloud a few of the openings to the class and brainstorm with them ideas of how each story could continue. Write some of the suggestions on the whiteboard. Then ask the children to take one of the openings from the photocopiable sheet and expand any of the ideas you came up with as a class or use their own ideas. They could just finish the sentence, or complete a whole paragraph – perhaps it will inspire a new story!

Story Openings

I woke up and immediately knew something was wrong...

Early one morning...

I promised myself I'd never go there again...

I had seen that strange old woman again...

It was a bright sunny day when Jack woke up, but...

"Don't play in the woods," Mum always said...

"Run for it!"...

"Just jump"...

Something in the box made a noise...

One day, a parcel arrived at Cherry Tree Primary School...

During the night Jo could hear a strange whining noise coming from outside...

Connor had a secret and he was determined that no one else would find out...

Gilbert did not believe in aliens...

When the dragon first came to St. Paul's Primary School, everyone thought that it was a strange sort of dog...

Mrs. Hardcaster was the latest Year 6 teacher...

Thunder rumbled and so too did Gary's stomach...

She stared at the burger in fascination...

The old King had only a short while to live...

Sunil had never believed in trolls...

The old house at the end of the road held a secret...

45. Story Endings

For the whole class.

Equipment:

- the photocopiable page **(Story Endings)**
- a whiteboard and a whiteboard pen for you
- writing journals and pencils for the children
- a range of stories that the class know well

Skills Developed:

- generating well-defined endings for stories

How to Play the Game

Give each child the photocopiable sheet **(Story Endings)** on the next page. Read aloud a few of the endings to the class and brainstorm with them ideas of how each one could continue. Write some of the suggestions on the whiteboard. Then ask the children to take one of the endings from the photocopiable sheet and expand any of the ideas you came up with as a class or use their own ideas. They could just finish the sentence, or complete a whole paragraph.

Once an ending has been completed, invite the children to create the whole story that leads to this ending. This could be mapped first, told and retold before being written. It is always interesting to see how a whole class creates stories that all lead to the same ending.

> **TIP**: Investigate how endings are written in books. Generally the writer shows what the main character has learnt or how they have changed. Often there is a link back to the beginning of the story, showing what has changed.

Story Endings

Finally, we were back home and Mum said to me, "...

I knew then that I'd never again...

Hameed knew that after this adventure, he would...

I had learnt an important lesson that day...

Lily smiled and thought about all that had happened...

Home had never looked more inviting...

The giant lay down and fell asleep...

At that moment, sun broke through the dark clouds...

After that, the door closed and was never opened again...

Eventually, they found the snow stone, but that is another story...

...and like the pages of a book, the doors closed shut...

The bell rang for the end of the day...

No one in the family ever spoke about what had happened, but sometimes, when the wind whispered in the trees,

Joanna thought back to what had happened and wished to see her friend just one more time...

...and a second later, they were indeed back in school...

"Of course," they promised – but some promises just itch to be broken...

"Never again," sighed the giant's wife, shaking her huge head...

At least, she had found a friend...

Sunlight lit up the edges of the storm clouds as the dragon spread its vast wings...

... and if you listen on a summer's evening you might just hear the faint sound of laughter, drifting over the moor...

They dragged the little boat up the beach and stared out to sea, but there was nothing there...

46. Finish the Story

For the whole class organised into pairs and then working independently.

Equipment:
- the photocopiable page **(Tiny and the Ogre)**
- writing journals and pencils for the children
- a short story or novel (for the Variation)

Skills Developed:
- completing a story

How to Play the Game

This final game is an invitation for children to completely finish a story that has been started (more substantially than the *Story Openings*). There are various ways that they might do this, but here are some ideas:

- talk it thought with a partner
- draw a story map or mountain
- complete a storyboard or mountain
- act it out and see what happens

Give the children a copy of the photocopiable sheet **(Tiny and the Ogre)** on the next page.

Once a basic plot has been thought about, the children could work in pairs to begin to orally create a rough first version. It's best to break the story up into 'chunks' or sections, with the pair rehearsing each one. Generally children need to retell stories at least three times before the tale begins to become more fluent.

Once they can tell a pretty fluent version they are ready to move into writing the full version of the story into their journals.

> **TIP**: Draw on what the children know about character development, dilemma and leading to a well-defined ending.

Variation
- Try playing the same game but use a story opening from a short story or novel. This is an interesting way to start a unit of work built around a novel. They will be intrigued to see what the author did with the story.

Tiny and the Ogre

The day that Poppy thought she saw an ogre was the first day of the summer holidays. It was walking down the alley at the back of the house where Poppy lived.

At first, Poppy noticed the shadow. Then she felt the ground shuddering. Finally, she heard the huge, heavy crunch of giant footsteps coming down the alleyway.

Poppy stood on tiptoes and looked out of the bathroom window. She caught a glimpse of the ogre's head as it passed by the back of the house. Amongst its vast head of hair, bushes grew and tiny trees sprouted. She could see birds' nests wobbling. Several crows cawed as they flew in and out of the ogre's forest of hair.

Poppy froze, ducked down and waited. Her heart thumped. The ogre thudded past and made its way down towards the park. When she dared to peek over the window-sill, the ogre had disappeared.

Of course, nobody believed her. Her Mum thought that she was making it up. Her father didn't even hear what she was saying. He just grunted.

Only Tiny believed her. Tiny had come to the school a few weeks before. He was the smallest person that Poppy had ever met. Until he arrived, Poppy had been the shortest person in her year group, but the day that Tiny arrived everything changed. He walked into the classroom with Mrs. Jenkins and everyone fell silent. Tiny looked so frail that a puff of wind might have blown him away. But what Tiny lacked in size, he made up for in other ways. And after Poppy had seen the ogre, she soon found out that whilst Tiny may have been small he also had strength...

UNIT 5: POETRY STARTERS 💿 📷

This section includes a range of poem starters to use with the children to encourage basic invention of new ideas and sentences so that they can begin to write their own poems.

Equipment:
- the photocopiable page **(Poetry Starters)**
- the audio CD and a CD player
- a whiteboard and a whiteboard pen for you
- pens and a roll of wallpaper for the children
- the image CD and an interactive whiteboard (for the Variation)

Skills Developed:
- playing with words and ideas
- using similes, metaphors, personification, alliteration and word play

How to Play the Game

This activity involves using a repeating phrase like a coat hanger to hang children's ideas from and create a poem. Give the children a copy of the photocopiable sheet **(Poetry Starters)** on page 94 and then introduce the session by listening to the ideas on the CD. Next, work together as a class to complete some of the poetry starters.

Children can then have a go on their own. There are many ways to do this, but it works very well using a roll of wallpaper with each starter written down. This could be pinned up or laid flat on the floor in the hall. Children can then use felt tips to write their thoughts under each starter.

<u>Example</u>

In the world of wonder *I saw leaves like frail, green skeletons.* *In the world of wonder* *I saw buses floating on the ocean waves.*
Last night I dreamed *That clouds were candyfloss carpets.* *Last night I dreamed* *That there was a goblin in the fridge!*
When the clock struck 13, *The walls became raspberry jelly.* *When the clock struck 13,* *The tables and chairs grew legs and walked away.*
In the future there will be *A pencil that can automatically spell.* *In the future there will be* *A purse that never runs out of money.*
I am a cat, *Slipping through the night.* *I am a hawk,* *Hovering at the roadside.* *I am a lion,* *Prowling in the heat.*

Of course, you can create additional starters for children to complete. A simple enough poetry frame for Year 2 children might be to make a list of magical wishes, using the opening, *I wish I was...* and then adding on their idea.

Variations

- For other ideas in this vein, see *The Poetry Pack* by Pie Corbett and Michaela Morgan. Not only are there poems to use, but also a handy set of images as well as an audio CD of poems read aloud.

- Try using some of the images on the CD as starting points for more descriptive writing. Show children how to list details in an image and then write descriptive lines for each one.

Poetry Starters

1. **Create an imaginary world.**
   In the world of wonder I saw/I found/I heard/I touched/I tasted/I captured/
   I imagined...

2. **Write about your dreams.**
   Last night I dreamed...

3. **Change one thing into another.**
   When the clock struck 13,
   The... became a...

4. **Write about amazing inventions from the future.**
   In the future there will be... which can....

5. **Choose an animal to become and say how you behave.**
   I am a cat...

UNIT 6: STORY BANK 💿

You can use these stories and the teaching notes with your class. The same tellings of these stories also appear on the CD.

Jack and the Beanstalk

Once, not twice, but once upon a time there lived a poor widow who had a son called Jack.

One day she told Jack to sell Milky-White the cow at the market. So Jack walked and he walked and he walked until he came to a little old man.

"If you sell me your cow I'll give you not one, not two, not three, not four, but five magic beans," said the old man.

But when Jack got back his mother was furious and she threw those beans right out of the window.

Early next morning, Jack woke to find that the beans had grown into a beanstalk that was higher than the sky. So he climbed and he climbed and he climbed until at last he reached the sky. There he found a road and at the end was a giant's castle. He crept inside.

Inside was the giant's wife. "Quick, hide in the oven. My husband is coming," she whispered, opening the greasy oven door. Jack hid.

Sure enough, along came the giant with three bags of gold, thumping, thumping, thumping.

"What's that I smell?" he roared. "Fee-fi-fo-fum, I smell the blood of an Englishman. Be he alive or be he dead, I'll use his bones to grind my bread."

Luckily, the giant then fell fast asleep. Hoping the giant would not catch him, Jack crept out of the oven, grabbed the gold, climbed down the beanstalk and escaped. His mother was mightily pleased.

But in the end, the gold ran out so Jack climbed and he climbed and he climbed till at last he reached the giant's castle.

Inside was the giant's wife. "Quick, hide in the oven. My husband is coming," she whispered, opening the greasy oven door. Jack hid.

Sure enough, along came the giant again with his hen that laid golden eggs, thumping, thumping, thumping.

"What's that I smell?" he roared. "Fee-fi-fo-fum, I smell the blood of an Englishman. Be he alive or be he dead, I'll use his bones to grind my bread."

Luckily, the giant fell fast asleep again, snoring like thunder. Hoping the giant would not catch him, Jack crept out of the oven, grabbed the hen, climbed down the beanstalk and escaped. His mother was mightily pleased.

But in the end, Jack was not content so he climbed and he climbed and he climbed till at last he reached the giant's castle.

Inside was the giant's wife. "Quick, hide in the oven. My husband is coming," she whispered, opening the greasy oven door. Jack hid.

Sure enough, along came the giant again with his golden harp, thumping, thumping, thumping.

"What's that I smell?" he roared. "Fee-fi-fo-fum, I smell the blood of an Englishman. Be he alive or be he dead, I'll use his bones to grind my bread."

Luckily, the giant fell asleep, snoring like thunder. Hoping the giant would not catch him, Jack crept out of the oven, grabbed the harp, and began to run. But the harp called out, "Master! Master!" and woke the giant up.

Jack climbed down and down and down the beanstalk, but the giant followed him. As soon as Jack reached the bottom, he called out, "Mother, bring me an axe."

So Jack chopped the beanstalk not once, not twice, but three times. The giant felt the stalk shake and quiver till he began to topple down and the beanstalk came toppling after.

So the giant broke his crown and Jack – why, he married a princess and they lived happily ever after.

Jack and the Beanstalk – Teaching Notes

Context/History

It is useful to know a little about the context or history of the stories that you are working on with the class. There is plenty of research you can carry out on the internet – though as always, be careful. But, you never know, your class may be newly inspired to invent their own stories through finding out where others came from!

Benjamin Tabart's 1807 telling of this story is the first version in print. There is also a version of *Jack and the Beanstalk* in Joseph Jacobs' 1890 English Fairytales book, based on a story told to him by his nursemaid in 1860. Jacobs' version is said to more closely adhere to the oral version, as it is less moralising than Tabart's version.

Introducing the Story

You need a fun and inventive way to introduce learning the story. It is no use saying, "Now we are going to work on the story of *Jack and the Beanstalk*." BORING ALARM BELLS will ring in the children's heads! Here are some creative ideas for exploring the story and setting the scene.

- 'Discover' a handful of beans you have hidden in the class. Then plant the beans with the children and let them watch them grow over the weeks you work with the story.

- Arrange for another teacher to knock at the door and explain to the class that they have heard someone has a prize cow to sell. Children could then suggest their best offer for the cow.

- Find some harp music to play to the children. Even better, if you know someone who plays the harp, ask them to come in and play for the class!

- Put up posters around the school advertising the cow.

- Enact the opening scene of the story in assembly, with you and other teachers taking various roles!

IMITATION – Learning the Story Well

Let the children listen to the story on the CD. Engage the children with discussion after they've heard the story – what do they think of it? What are their favourite bits? Which bits don't they like? After this, make sure you draw a class story map and invent some actions so that they become familiar with the key elements of the story and can begin to tell it themselves. This story is probably too long for younger or less experienced tellers to learn it word-for-word, so they should practise retelling it in their own words. However, because of its repetitive nature, it should be possible for older children to learn this version.

Here are some ideas you can use with the children for getting to know the story really well.

- A fun starter activity for learning the story is to get the whole class learning the rhyme *Fee-fi-fo-fum*. You could split the class in two and have a competition to see which side of the class is loudest at chanting the rhyme. Vary this by challenging each group to hiss it the quietest – who is the scariest?

- The story lends itself to being split into chunks. You could organise the class into groups and give each group a different chunk to learn. They could then come together as a class and retell the full story, with each group responsible for telling their chunk.

- Role-play activities. You could set up scenarios from the story for the children to act out – or try any of these ideas to explore the story further.

  - Play Gossiping over the Gate (see page 32) with this story. Jack's Mum and his neighbour could have a gossip about what naughty Jack has been up to and how tall the beanstalk has grown.

  - Play Agony Aunt (see page 34). This can be from anyone's perspective. How about from the perspective of the worried giant's wife who keeps finding a human boy in her kitchen? Or the giant who thinks his wife is lying to him because he can constantly smell a human, but she swears no human enters the house?

- Why not recreate the market place where Jack sold the cow. Children can act out a discussion between some eyewitnesses who have seen Jack sell the cow for beans. Why on earth did he do that? Who was that strange person with the beans who bought the cow?

- The class could act out a trial scene that happens 'after' the story. Encourage the children to engage in debate – was Jack right to steal from the giant? Was Jack right to kill the giant?

- Children could draw pictures based around key elements of the story, e.g. *a picture or map showing how huge the giant's kitchen is and how small Jack is in comparison, or a picture or sculpture showing how big the beanstalk is.*

- The class could write a menu for what the giant's wife cooks in the kitchen (perhaps it is dragon stew!).

INNOVATION – Changing the Story

Once the class know the story really well, you can model how to change elements of the story so that the children can begin to create their own 'innovations'. Begin very simply, making basic changes to the story map by crossing out and changing bits so that it's very clear to the children what you are doing.

Here are some very simple ways that the story could be changed.

- Change a character's name – instead of Jack, perhaps the main character could be a girl called Julia.
- Change the animal – instead of a cow, perhaps it is a prize sheep, with the softest wool in the land.
- Change the baddie – instead of a giant, it could be another fairy tale creature, such as a troll, or a talking dragon.
- Change the magical object – instead of beans, the main character could be given sunflower seeds which grow up to the sun.
- Change other objects in the story – instead of a golden harp, it could be a golden trumpet.

Once the class has understood how make these simple changes, move on to more complex innovations. Here are some ideas.

- Change what Jack gets in exchange for his cow and where he is transported to – instead of magic beans, Jack could be given an old spade that he puts in the garden and overnight it has dug a huge hole to a forbidden cave and a ladder has appeared leading down to it! In order to kill the giant who lives in the cave, Jack must push down the ladder as the giant chases him.

- Change further characters and their role in the story – instead of the giant's wife, it could be the daughter of the house who Jack falls in love with and has to rescue too!

- Modernise the story – the beanstalk could become a telegraph pole and Jack could be breaking and entering into a royal Palace!

Remember, the story of Jack is simply about someone who enters a forbidden place three times, is helped to hide by someone, then steals from the owner of the place he has broken into, finally defeating him! Use this basic story framework to create new stories. Parts of the story can always be changed, e.g. *the story could end with a reconciliation and not a murder.*

The Pied Piper of Hamelin

This is the story of The Pied Piper of Hamelin and this is the way that I tell it.

In the year 1284, in the town of Hamelin, there was a plague of rats. They had rats in the ditches, rats on the floor, rats in the houses and rats in their britches! Even the cats had left!

But that year, a stranger came to Hamelin, dressed in a long flowing coat of many colours. Some people said it was Joseph, but soon he had become known as Brightman. He said that he could get rid of the rats for the right sum of money. The elders of the town agreed to pay him if only he could rid them of the rats.

Brightman took out his pipe and began to play and the rats streamed out of the houses to follow him. Rats, rats, everywhere, following Brightman out of the town, across the hills, squealing and squeaking till they came to the River Weser. Brightman strode into the river and the rats followed, only to drown!

That afternoon Brightman returned to the town, but the elders refused to pay him any money. Now the days they ran by like rabbits and the elders tried to pretend that the rats had not been that much of a problem.

A week later Brightman returned to Hamelin dressed in a scarlet cloak, wearing a strange mask. One last time, he asked for his money. One last time, they refused. So he took out his pipe and played again. But this time, a different tune. This time it was not rats that followed him, it was the children. Children, children everywhere, chattering and chortling following Brightman up into the mountains.

And they were never seen again.

The Pied Piper of Hamelin – Teaching Notes

Context/History

The earliest mention of this story appears to have been on a stained glass window placed in the Church of Hamelin c.1300. Goethe, the Brothers Grimm and Robert Browning have all written versions of the tale. The legend has been around for many years, but was developed into a full narrative in the 16th Century. Many believe it was based on the horrific Children's Crusade in the Middle Ages which is a piece of history children may be interested in learning about.

Introducing the Story

You need a fun and inventive way to introduce learning the story that will grab your class's attention. Here are some creative ideas for exploring the story and setting the scene.

- A strong feature of this story is an abundance of rats, so perhaps you could begin by showing the class photos or videos of rats and discussing their impression of rats. What would it be like if they had an infestation of rats? Even better if you can bring a live pet rat into the class – though check if this is allowed!

- Another important aspect of the story is the music the Pied Piper plays. Perhaps you can you play a recording of a haunting pipe? Or do some of the children play recorders so that they can create the sound?

- You could act in role as the mayor and say the school has had an infestation of rats – what solution do the class have?

- You could read some of Robert Browning's poem *The Pied Piper of Hamelin*.

- Play 'follow my leader' to bring alive for the children the method Brightman used to rid the town of rats.

IMITATION – Learning the Story Well

Let the children listen to the story on the CD. Engage the children with discussion after they've heard the story – what do they think of it? What are their favourite bits? Which bits don't they like? After this, make sure you draw story maps and invent some actions so that they become familiar with the key elements of the story and can begin to tell it themselves. If the children are experienced, this is probably a story they can learn word-for-word, though many will be confident enough to embellish and use their own words from the start.

Here are some ideas you can use with the children for getting to know the story really well.

- The most important part of learning a story is constant discussion around the ideas of the story. As a class, make a list of questions about the story that you want to know the answer to. Some of these may include:

    - why does the Pied Piper wear a coat of different colours?
    - why does he return to Hamelin wearing a mask?
    - what has happened to the children?
    - what is the moral of the story?
    - who was right – the elders, or the Pied Piper, or no one?

- Role-play activities. You could set up scenarios from the story for the children to act out – or try any of these ideas to explore the story further.

    - Play Agony Aunt (see page 34). On the CD you hear a phone conversation between the Mayor and an Agony Aunt – children could have a go at this themselves.

    - Some children could act in role as elders from the town interviewing strangers (played by other volunteers) who claim that they can deal with the rat problem. What does each of them offer? Why do they pick the Pied Piper in the end?

    - Children could act out the scene when the rats are first discovered and what the townspeople discuss as a first solution.

The ENORMOUS Book of Talk for Writing Games for KS2

- In the hall, act out the Pied Piper leading all the rats away from the town. Have a child who can play the recorder play the role of the Pied Piper and the children playing the rats could play the rats and wear rat masks that they have made.

- Make a list of reasons WHY the elders of Hamelin have refused to pay the Pied Piper. Follow this up by inviting children to act out a council meeting discussing it and using the list to drive the drama.

- Children could draw pictures based around key elements of the story, e.g. *a picture of the Pied Piper's beautiful coat or the mask that he wears when he returns to the town.*

INNOVATION – Changing the Story

Once the class know the story really well, you can model how to change elements of the story so that the children can begin to create their own 'innovations'. Begin very simply, making basic changes to the story map by crossing out and changing bits so that it's very clear to the children what you are doing.

Here are some very simple ways that the story could be changed.

- Change a character's name – the Pied Piper could be known by a name other than Brightman.

- Change the name of the town to something else – instead of Hamelin, perhaps it could be the name of the place where your school is!

- Change the animals – instead of rats, why not change the infestation to another creature, such as snakes, locusts, pigeons, or even goblins?

- Change the object – instead of the Pied Piper playing the pipe, perhaps he could play another instrument, such as a violin, a guitar or a drum.

- Change other objects in the story – instead of a brightly coloured cape, there could be another item that Brightman is known for, such as a sparkly waistcoat, or some pointy shoes.

- Change the ending slightly – the Pied Piper could lead away the adults of the town instead of the children and he could lead them to another place, such as into the forest.

Once the class has understood how to make these simple changes, move on to more complex innovations. Here are some ideas.

- Modernise the story...

  - It could be set in a large modern city, such as New York, which has been infested by monsters. The politicians might pay a superhero to exterminate them, but then do not thank him when he has done so!

  - Alternatively, perhaps it is set it in a school that has a problem that the main character fixes, but then the school treats them badly and doesn't repay them, so they seek revenge!

Remember, at its simplest, *The Pied Piper of Hamelin* is a story about someone who helps people, is refused payment and this leads to a sad ending. Use this simple structure to come up with some more stories where a character does a good turn, but is then treated badly.

Too High – The Story of Icarus

And so it was that Daedalus, the renowned inventor, found himself dragged before the great King Minos, in the dead of night with the rush lights flickering.

"You!" roared the King. "You are the one who built the Labyrinth. You are the one who led to my Ariadne being taken away by Theses. It is your fault!"

"But your majesty, you asked me to build the Labyrinth…"

"No buts – take him and his snivelling son to the tower."

And so it was that Icarus found himself dragged to the tower in the dead of night, up the winding steps and into the top room.

Every morning the oak door would open and a bowl of food and a loaf of bread would be shoved into the room. Once a week a new candle would be provided so that at night they were not in complete darkness.

Icarus would pace up and down ranting and raving about what he would say to the King. But Daedalus spent his time leaning on the window sill, staring out across the city towards the distant hills of Crete and the sea that lay like a thin blue ribbon in the distance.

Daedalus would look down the sheer sides of the tower to the people far below who scurried about their daily business like so many ants.

And one day he looked up at the great buzzards as they wheeled high in the sky, caught on the thermals, spiralling upwards and he saw a feather falling. Daedalus snatched the feather and as he held it in the palm of his hand he had an idea. At first, just the seed of an idea, but it soon took root.

Daedalus gathered the candle stubs and hoarded them, so that at night they had to sit in the darkness. He took the bread and crumbled it, scattering the crumbs on the window sill. At first the sparrows came fluttering down. Later, the white finches and magpies. Some days he used to lure down the buzzards with small pieces of meat. And whenever a bird landed, Daedalus would lean out and 'snitch', he would grab a feather.

When the pile of feathers was enough, he melted the wax in the midday sun and used it to bind together the feathers into two mighty pairs of wings. He tore his shirt into strips and made bindings so they could attach the wings.

Early one morning, as the sun rose and before the guards were awake, Daedalus strapped the wings onto Icarus and himself. They stood then on the edge of the window ledge, toes curled over the side, holding hands.

"Whatever happens Icarus, keep gliding straight – don't let a thermal catch you and send you too high. The sun is too hot for our wings to last. At first we'll dip down so hold your arms firm and we shall glide across the sea towards Sardinia and towards safety."

Without warning, he tugged Icarus and they swooped down and as the air filled their wings they straightened up and began to glide over the city, across the hills and above the sea.

"I can fly, I can fly," yelled Icarus with excitement, but Daedalus just tightened his grip on his son's hand. But full of freedom, having escaped Minos, Icarus was in no mood for heeding his father's sense and he let go of his father's hand, swooping and dipping and diving – looping the loop, till a thermal caught him and Icarus began to spiral upwards.

"Glide straight," yelled Daedalus, but already Icarus was too far from his father's calling, spiralling up and up. So high, so certain, so full of himself that he did not hear the steady drip, drip, drip. Nor did he notice the feathers falling till in one moment he hung in the air, no longer circling upwards and then in the next moment he dropped like a rock, plummeting down towards the sea and Icarus saw the blues and the greens and the white crests of the waves rush up to meet him.

And Daedalus too saw his son fall, 'crack' into the sea! And Daedalus, he glided on to Sardinia, with his heart heavier than lead, knowing that his own son had died by his own invention, by his own invention…

And that is the end of the story of Daedalus the inventor and Icarus who flew too high, too high, too high…

Too High – The Story of Icarus – Teaching Notes

Context/History

Introduce the class to the history of the story – of course, if you are already studying the Greeks, or have studied the Greek myths before, this will help! Icarus' story was often alluded to by Greek poets, but the first lengthy version is found in Ovid's *Metamorphoses* (43BC). Take a look at the myths that come before Icarus – the building of the Labyrinth to imprison the Minotaur, and Ariadne helping Theseus escape the Labyrinth with a ball of string.

Introducing the Story

You need a fun and inventive way to introduce learning the story that will grab your class's attention. Here are some creative ideas for exploring the story and setting the scene.

- If you are studying the Greeks, this would be the perfect time to tie in learning the story of *Icarus*. If not, perhaps you could give a short history of the Greeks, their myths and then explore one of the most famous myths of all.

- Bring in different types of feathers and ask the class which would make the best pair of wings. Have a look at some pictures or videos of birds, noting their wing-span and how they fly.

- You could show the children some candles and wax dripping and ask them for ideas of what the wax could be made into.

- The story centres around the idea of flying to freedom. Show the class *YouTube* videos of the first attempts by people to fly without a plane. Discuss how you would make a great flying machine!

- There are many beautiful classical paintings of Icarus and his wings that you can find on the internet and show the class.

IMITATION – Learning the Story Well

Let the children listen to the story on the CD. Engage the children with discussion after they've heard the story – what do they think of it? What are their favourite bits? Which bits don't they like? After this, make sure you draw story maps and invent some actions so that they become familiar with the key elements of the story and can begin to tell it themselves. This story is too long for the class to learn word-for-word, so they should practise being able to retell it in their own words.

Here are some ideas you can use with the children for getting to know the story really well.

- The story lends itself to being split into chunks. You could organise the class into groups and give each group a different chunk to learn. They could then come together as a class and retell the full story, with each group responsible for telling their chunk.

- The most important part of learning a story is constant discussion around the ideas of the story. As a class, you could talk about.

  - Being imprisoned – discuss with the class what tactics and inventions they might use to escape from somewhere and how they might occupy their time if they were imprisoned.

  - What the children would do if they were trapped – how would they pass the time if all they had was some bread, candles and clothes? Perhaps find some great, true escape stories and share these with the class.

- Come up with ideas of 'thoughts in the head in the tower'. These are the private thoughts inside the heads of Daedalus and Icarus when they are imprisoned. They will probably be quite different – Daedalus is the logical older inventor, whereas Icarus is young and impulsive!

- The children could write instruction poems with the title 'How To Make a Magical Pair of Wings'. They could draw pictures or create 3-D models to accompany these.

- Challenge the class to design their own flying machines. They could create labelled drawings of them with accompanying explanations of how they work.

- Children could also draw pictures of other inventions that might be found in Daedalus' Inventor's Laboratory.

- Ask the class to create newspaper spreads (with pictures) detailing different points of the story, e.g. *DAEDALUS IMPRISONED! DAEDALUS ESCAPES!* This story would also be a good one for the children to draw as a cartoon.

- Role-play activities. You could set up scenarios from the story for the children to act out – or try any of these ideas to explore the story further.

    - Why not perform the story around different spaces in the school as a site-specific promenade production? Poppy went on a storytelling course with renowned storytellers Hugh Lupton and Daniel Morden where each storyteller took a section of the story of *Odysseus* and performed it in a different space around the Welsh hills at Cae Mabon, a storytelling centre. By giving the children control over where they perform their sections, this will make them feel they have ownership of the story and make it really special. Try and think of places around/in the school that would fit with the story! Let them act out sections in groups.

    - Children could act out a new scene related to the story, e.g. *a scene of the fishermen on the beach claiming to have seen two people flying out of a tower and across the sea. Another new scene children could improvise would be between King Minos and one of his advisors – was he right to banish them to the tower? Does he trust his guards to keep them trapped in there?*

    - Play Gossiping over the Gate (see page 32) with this story. On the CD we play the roles of two guards gossiping about what has happened to Daedalus and Icarus.

    - The children could make puppets of characters from the story and perform a puppet show.

    - Arrange the children in pairs to play the roles of Daedalus and Icarus when they are imprisoned in the tower room at night. Use solemn music and make the classroom dark to set the scene. Children should then improvise the dialogue between the two characters.

    - Have the children present a news story, reporting on the events in the story.

INNOVATION – Changing the Story

Once the class know the story really well, you can model how to change elements of the story so that the children can begin to create their own 'innovations'. Begin very simply, making basic changes to the story map by crossing out and changing bits so that it's very clear to the children what you are doing.

Here are some very simple ways that the story could be changed.

- Change the character names, genders and relationship – instead of a father and a son, you could have a mother and a daughter, or a grandfather and granddaughter.

- Change an element of the opening – the King could accuse Daedalus of something other than building the Labyrinth.

- Change an object – instead of a loaf of bread, the guards could give them a block of cheese.

- Change a scene – rather than being trapped in the tower Daedalus and Icarus could be trapped in a castle. Children could also change the country where it is set. Although it may seem strange changing the location of a classic Greek myth, it is important to do so, so that children have the courage to adapt stories for themselves.

Once the class has understood how to make these simple changes, move on to more complex innovations. Here are some ideas.

- Change an element of the plot – instead of Daedalus coming up with the idea to escape, it could be the younger character of Icarus who comes up with the idea, and the older character who does not heed the warning at the end. Alternatively, perhaps Icarus flying too close to the sun at the end could be the result of an accidental gust of wind, and not because he did not heed his father's advice.

- Change the way that Daedalus and Icarus escape where they are – perhaps they do not invent something, perhaps someone helps them.

- Change the genre of the story – perhaps the story could be set in a fantasy world where Daedalus invents a magic spell to help them escape.

- Why not change the story so that it has a happy ending? There could be a reconciliation between the protagonists and the King who has trapped them.

- Modernise the tale. Give the characters current names. Perhaps Daedalus could build a new shopping centre in an area of outstanding beauty which has led to his and Icarus being confined to a room in a tower block.

Remember, this story has a simple five part structure to it:

1. the accusation from the villain
2. the two main characters imprisoned and complaining of their fate
3. the idea of how to escape
4. the escape sequence
5. the consequence of the escape

Use this simple structure to create a completely different story. Most children will be able to relate to superheroes whose powers are often a burden to them. Children will need to think about who accuses who? Where are the main characters imprisoned? How do they plan an escape? What happens when they do escape?

Midas

Early one morning, the gardeners in King Midas's palace found Silenus sleeping in the rose gardens. He was snoring like thunder. So they bound him hand and foot with flowers and vines and dragged him before the King.

At first, Midas was cross, but Silenus enchanted him with wonderful stories of journeys made past frightening whirlpools to magical cities where the fruit of youth grew. Midas sat spellbound for five whole days. In the end, Silenus returned to his home and the god Dionysus granted Midas one wish to reward his hospitality. At once, Midas said, "Pray, grant that all I touch be turned into gold."

At first this seemed like a good idea. He turned stones to gold, then a table and chairs, but when he sat down to eat the food, it turned to gold. Then he tried to take a sip of water, and of course, that too turned into liquid gold. Now the days they rolled by and Midas was surrounded by gold, but he grew thinner and thinner. Why, he dared not touch his wife, let alone his children, in case he turned them into statues.

In the end, Midas pleaded with Dionysus to free him from the curse, the curse of his own greed. Dionysus flung back his head and laughed. He told Midas to bathe in the source of the river Pactolus which to this very day still has specks of gold on its sandy banks. Now you would have thought that Midas had learnt not to fool around with the gods, but he went to a musical contest between Apollo and Marsyas. When Apollo won, Midas began to argue, shouting and yelling at the umpire who happened to be a River-god. He was punished with a pair of donkey's ears!

Now King Midas he felt so ashamed that he pulled on a cap and kept the ears hidden from sight. But of course his hair grew and it grew till in the end he had to visit his barber. Midas threatened the man with death if he told anyone, but you know how secrets are, they have a way of sneaking out, and in the end the barber found it was impossible to keep the King's shameful secret to himself, he just had to tell somebody...

So late one night, when no one was looking, the barber crept to the riverbank and he dug a hole. When nobody was about, he whispered into the hole, "King Midas has the ears of a donkey!" Then he filled the hole and went away feeling much better. Unfortunately, a reed sprouted from the hole and when the wind blew it whispered the secret. It whispered those words to all who passed by, "King Midas has the ears of a donkey!" So, once again Midas felt the sting of shame.

Midas – Teaching Notes

Context/History

If your class have learnt *Icarus*, or another Greek myth, *King Midas* would be a good one to follow, as this is also a Greek myth. It is also an ideal story to work with if your class is studying the Greeks. A lengthy version of the myth can be found in Ovid's *Metamorphoses*. Ovid wrote the basic stories down in *Metamorphoses*, about 2,000 years ago though the tales are probably far older. Learning about the god Dionysus who gives Midas his gold 'gift' would be worthwhile.

Introducing the Story

You need a fun and inventive way to introduce learning the story that will grab your class's attention. Here are some creative ideas for exploring the story and setting the scene.

- Bring in some gold or gold-sprayed items, such as a sprayed fern or leaves. Discuss impressions of gold and why some people may desire gold.

- Put posters up around the school advertising the arrival of Dionysus: *Have your one wish granted! Dionysus in town today! What will you wish for?*

- Arrange for another teacher to come into class and start the rumour that the head teacher has been seen wearing a pair of donkey ears! Discuss with the children how this would affect their view of him/her.

IMITATION – Learning the Story Well

Let the children listen to the story on the CD. Engage the children with discussion after they've heard the story – what do they think of it? What are their favourite bits? Which bits don't they like? After this, make sure you draw story maps and invent some actions so that they become familiar with the key elements of the story and can begin to tell it themselves in their own words.

Here are some ideas you can use with the children for getting to know the story really well.

- The story lends itself to being split into chunks. You could organise the class into groups and give each group a different chunk to learn. They could then come together as a class and retell the full story, with each group responsible for telling their chunk.

- The most important part of learning a story is constant discussion around the ideas of the story. As a class you could talk about:

  - what wonderful tales the old satyr Silenus could tell the King – what stories of magical cities, magical creatures and people might he have told to enchant Midas for five whole days? Discuss with the class what their favourite stories are that they could listen to over and over again.

  - 'the Midas touch' – would it be a good thing if everything you touch turned into gold? The children might reach the conclusion, like the King in this story, that everything being gold would have its drawbacks – they may not appreciate their Mum or dog turning to gold! To follow on from this, discuss with the children more broadly what other wishes might also be burdens.

  - superpowers – if the children could have one special power, like turning things to gold, what superpower would they have?

- Make a class story book, all contributing one story for Midas that Silenus might tell.

- The 'ears' story has other versions from India and Wales (King March's ears) – see if you can find them on the internet and read them to the class.

- Encourage the class to write 'wish' poems with each line starting *I wish...* detailing their magical wishes.

- Bring something gold in and ask the children to write a descriptive paragraph about what it looks and feels like.

- Role-play activities. You could set up scenarios from the story for the children to act out – or try any of these ideas to explore the story further.

  - Why not recreate the scene where Midas pleads with Dionysus to free him from the curse?

  - Children could act out a new scene related to the story, e.g. *Midas goes to his local shopping centre, but everything he touches turns to gold.* They can explore what havoc this causes.

  - Play Gossiping over the Gate (see page 32) with this story. Children could be in role as the Queen and her maid and have a gossip about what has happened to the King. Alternatively, the servants could be discussing what they think is going on.

  - Perhaps you could play 'Whispers' where someone quietly whispers a rumour to the next person, if it's whispered quietly enough – the rumour may change through people not hearing it correctly! It is best if you give the rumour, and it is related to the story, so no feelings are hurt by a nasty rumour!

INNOVATION – Changing the Story

Once the class know the story really well, you can model how to change elements of the story so that the children can begin to create their own 'innovations'. Begin very simply, making basic changes to the story map by crossing out and changing bits so that it's very clear to the children what you are doing.

Here are some very simple ways that the story could be changed.

- Change the characters – instead of King Midas, the story could be about a Queen, the character of Silenus could be changed and it could be a different god who grants Midas his wish.

- Change a scene – rather than bathing in a river to cure him of his golden gift, Midas could be instructed to do something else, such as bathe in a lake or bathe in milk. Instead of the barber whispering the secret of the ears into a hole in the riverbank, it could be whispered into a hole in a tree and the leaves could carry the secret, as they blow away in the wind.

- Change an event – instead of donkey's ears, Midas could be punished with something else, e.g. *a cat's tail!*

- Change the superpower that Midas is given. What if everything he touched disappeared, or turned to water?

Once the class has understood how make these simple changes, move on to more complex innovations. Here are some ideas.

- Midas could do another good deed to make Dionysus grant him a wish. For example, instead of showing hospitality to Silenus, he could shelter a poor beggar from a storm, who turns out to be a god in disguise.

- Modernise the tale – the protagonist could show kindness to someone who turns out to be an important person, like a politician.

- Change the genre – instead of a myth, children could make this into a fantasy tale where the protagonist helps someone who turns out to be a magician and puts a spell upon them.

- Read aloud the passage from Narnia where the lion Aslan breathes on the stone creatures and makes them come to life. Seeing a similar idea in another story may give your pupils ideas about how they can adapt Midas and change the story.

Remember, at its simplest, *King Midas* is a story about someone who gets their wish, but their wish turns out to be a burden, so they ask to lose their gift. Use this simple structure to create a completely different story. Most children will be able to relate to superheroes whose powers are often a burden to them.

Notes

The ENORMOUS Book of Talk for Writing Games for KS2